SPIRALS

The Connection

DEBORAH GREENSPAN

Llumina Press

Cover: Deborah Greenspan

Copyright Deborah Greenspan 2010

This second edition was originally published as *InSight of God* under the pseudonym, Deborah Claire.

All rights reserved. No part of this publication may be reproduced or transmitted in any form or by any means electronic or mechanical, including photocopy, recording, or any information storage and retrieval system, without permission in writing from the publisher.

Requests for permission to make copies of any part of the work should be mailed to Permissions Department, Llumina Press, 7915 W. McNab Road, Tamarac, FL 33321

PB ISBN: 978-1-60594-588-0
HC ISBN: 978-1-60594-546-0
Printed in the United States of America

Library of Congress Cataloging-in-Publication Data

Greenspan, Deborah.
 Spirals : the Connection / by Deborah Greenspan.
   p. cm.
 ISBN 978-1-60594-588-0 (alk. paper)
 1. Spiritual life. I. Title.
BL624.G7335 2004
204'.4--dc22   2004012660

Printed in the United States

DEDICATION

This is dedicated to my children, Cassie and Jo, and to my mother, Clarice. Without their love, this book would still be banging around in my head.

Table of Contents

Prologue — **A Mystical Experience** — 1

The Center – **Inspiration** — 7

The First Spiral — **God & Goddess** — 13
- The Authors
- The Goddess
- The God
- Union of Goddess and God

The Second Spiral — **Life & Death** — 23
- The Stage
- Riding the River of Time
- Destination: Compassion
- Death?
- Rebirth
- The Role of Coincidence

The Third Spiral — **Men & Women** — 43
- The Actors
- Male vs Female Culture
- Dancing Together
- Mapping the Steps of the Dance
- And on and on . . .

The Fourth Spiral — **Power & Love** — 53
- The Conflict

Power in Relationships
Negotiating Power
The Balance of Power
    Give and Take Relationships
    Two Takers
    Faces to the Wall
So What Can We Do?

The Fifth Spiral — Good & Evil   75

Motivation
Rationalization
Beauty and Ugliness
Cultural Definitions of Good and Evil
Can Cultures Be Good or Bad?
Us and Them
Religion
Empathy and Compassion
Sex and Death
Fear and Hope
The Way of Love

The Sixth Spiral — Freedom & Responsibility   109

The Plot
Making Choices
Finding the Balance
The Tree of Life
Living Creatively

The Seventh Spiral — Epiphany   127

Ease and Dis-ease
Emotion and Health
Emotional Expression
The Balance Between Happiness and Disease

The Eighth Spiral — God and Self   **139**
     The Climax
     God Is Born
     The Divine Universe
     The Multiple Nature of Truth

Epilogue — Denouement   **149**
     Between Madness and Reason

INDEX   **156**

The Sum of All Things:

Spiral	Core Lesson	Dramatic Connection	Chakra	Color
The Center	Wholeness	Inspiration	All	Light
God & Goddess	Truth	Authors	Root	Red
Life & Death	Courage	The Stage	Sexual	Orange
Men & Women	Trust	Actors	Solar Plexus	Yellow
Power & Love	Generosity	Conflict	Heart	Green
Good & Evil	Hope	Motivation	Heart	Green
Freedom & Responsibility	Joy	The Plot	Throat	Blue
Ease & Dis-ease	Faith	Commitment	Third Eye	Indigo
God & Self	Self-Expression	Climax	Crown	Purple
Madness & Reason	Relativity	Manifestation	All	White

PROLOGUE

Even as a child I wanted to know everything. I was and am insatiably curious. Afraid of dying and horrified by all the contradictions in human behavior with which I was expected to live, I had many questions but no answers. How could it be that innocent children could get sick and die, but villains could survive and prosper? What made it possible for a man like Hitler to gain the power to destroy so many millions? Why did human beings never seem to agree about anything? What was all the fighting about? Why was peace so rare and misery so common? And, if there was a God, and He was all-knowing and all-powerful, how could anyone but He be responsible for the state of the world and the state of my consciousness?

One day, at the age of sixteen, I sat at the back of the school bus asking myself questions like these. Suddenly, the clamor of the other students faded out and the clamor in my head was perfectly still. In that timeless moment, I understood everything. I saw it all and it all made perfect sense. Everything, all the contradictions of life, related so simply, a tapestry woven of a million colors and textures. All of life, everything I had ever experienced, learned, and seen, fit together into a cohesive whole, and there were no more questions.

Underlying all the confusion, I saw, was a simple form, a structure deeply embedded in nature, which pulled everything into place. The universe, I realized, has design and purpose that we sometimes miss in all the seething turmoil.

It was as if I had seen God. I understood the number of creation, the rhythm of the cosmos, the Art of Life. I was awestruck. If the universe were a million disconnected words, I had seen the grammar that gave them meaning. If the world were a mass of random colors, I had seen the design that turned it into a painting. If all of creation could be described as music, I had seen the one sustaining rhythm that gave it unity and purpose. If Life were a story, I had seen the intention that made it live.

In that moment I became an artist. Of what kind I had no idea, for I had no particular talent. All I knew was that it was my purpose in life to find a way to express what I had seen, to pass along the understanding I had gained. I was only sixteen and didn't know how much pain I would suffer before I could even attempt to do that, so I was filled with hope and a kind of incandescent joy.

Everywhere I went and everything I did was ultimately focused on finding my way back to that original experience, on putting it into words so that I could explain it to others and to myself and, hopefully, to experience it again. Yet a secondhand telling could not recreate the moment, could not make it happen again. In fact, words seemed to make it smaller, to pull it down to earth, and that was not my intention. I wanted to share it;

I wanted others to know it with me. I tried music; I tried painting and sculpture; I tried drama.

I was filled with more questions than ever. What had happened to me? What was this experience all about? Where had it come from? Where had it gone? Why, when I tried to express it, did it become so small? What was it about words that was so limiting? Was I the only one who'd ever seen it, or did other people know it as well? Was it possible to relate it in a way that would open it up for others?

Though I wanted to write this book since the day it happened, it has taken me over thirty years to acquire the knowledge and wisdom needed to do so. I found the insight and inspiration at the age of sixteen, but it took years of living and learning, years of research, to reach the point where it has all come together in my life as it once came together, momentarily, in my head.

My study was conducted under the 'try it and see' theory of life. That is, I tried everything, gave myself over to every experience. I did everything I wanted to do and suffered the consequences. I have been a child, a wife, a businesswoman, a student, an artist, a worker, a thief, a mother, a daughter, a sister, a lover, a sexual slave, a victim, and a victor. I have been irresponsible and selfish, and responsible and kind. I have been disciplined and impulsive. I have been a worker and a boss, a giver and a taker, a student and a teacher. I've been rich, and I've been poor. I've been in love, and I've been alone.

I began my unorthodox college career in the '70's with an interest in science and medicine, and went from there to psychology and sociology to theatre, and finally, twenty years later to Communication, getting a bachelor's with thirty-four credits more than I needed, and a master's on top of that. In between, I must have read four or five thousand books. Though I never realized until after I began this book, everything I did, every feeling I felt, every person I met, every lesson I learned was grist for the mill, ground up and assimilated into the whole that I'd glimpsed that day on the bus.

I had seen, ever so briefly, that everything fit into the tapestry of life, that the universe— and therefore our lives as part of the universe—made sense and had meaning. Thus I knew that I could reject nothing. I had no standards, and every choice I made through the years was intended simply to keep my choices open. When I suffered it was usually because I felt stuck in some way, as if I'd spiraled down into some place where I had no choices. Bereft upon this shore, I would cry out at my fate, at the darkness inside me, and set out to free myself again. Or sometimes I would just cry helplessly until someone else came along and set me free.

I discovered that I was not alone, that there were many others who had had an experience like I'd had. I found and read voraciously the work of other writers who admitted to having been inspired by a vision. I came to know that the universe does make sense, that contradictions are not really contradictions, but just extremes of Truth. I understood that we are all adventurers on this world, all intent on reaching the place I'd glimpsed so fortuitously so many years ago. Every epiphany, every grace, every vision, and every dream, which transcends the little mainstream reality we usually accept as Reality, is an open door into Truth and a pathway to Joy. We are all mystics opening doors to heaven. This book, I hope, will help you open yours.

Recently—coincidentally, some might say—I discovered chaos[1], a mathematical theory that is already changing the world. While reading about this new science, I found that I too have been writing about chaos, the difference being that my lack of mathematical expertise requires me to use words rather than numbers to describe it. Chaos is the science of wholeness, of order beneath disorder; it pulls the universe together and looks at it globally, not as bits and pieces, recognizing that it makes sense.

My purpose has been to create a picture of the underlying order beneath the confusion we see everywhere, examining science, the natural world, human nature, and mysticism in this context. I have organized this work into eight main chapters, each looking at the tension between a pair of opposites, which I have defined as the foundation of reality as we know it. The first chapter paints a picture of this fundamental process and subsequent chapters explain how this opposition is reiterated over and over again in different areas of life.

I've correlated each chapter to a dramatic term: the inspiration, the authors, the stage, the actors etc. I've done this because human beings live in stories. Every event in our lives becomes part of the story we create to define who we are and who each person is in relation to us. Without a story to contain and structure our emotions, actions, reactions, and beliefs, we hang over a terrifying abyss of chaotic impressions. Stories are what make us human. Stories are the relational structure that keeps us sane (if sane we are).

Which comes first? The story or the reality? This chicken-or-egg question doesn't have an answer, and we might ask if it really matters. The fact is there is a correlation between drama and life and the line between them is blurred. Life *is* drama, and drama *is* life. It's just that in life, the boring and repetitive bits have been left in; there are too many plots and mini-climaxes to count, and the true ending is so far in the future, we don't see how it all ties back to the beginning. But it does, and because it does, the structures of drama can be applied to life.

By relating the spirals to the parts of a story, I hope to demystify these structures and show how they apply to our lives and, in particular, how they work together to make us what we are. Taken together, as a whole, this book pulls in on itself and returns us to the beginning. If you can see how it fits together at the end, then I have succeeded in expressing, at last, the vision that took over my life so many years ago.

THE CENTER

Inspiration

In the beginning, time was not a river flowing from then ... to now ... to hereafter; and life, as we know it, existing in space and in time did not exist. In the beginning, the universe was only the potential to be. Time and space were a sea—at once a great ocean of nothing ... and of everything: infinite and eternal, nonexistent and transitory.

All possibilities were in that eternal sea. Like a dream without substance and without form, shifting ... changing ... becoming and disappearing, all possibilities, all potentialities, rose and fell, were born and died, began and ended, before they began.

Nothing disturbed these primordial waters, no wind blew across the surface, for there was no surface; no earth rose up beneath, for there was no bottom. In truth, there were no waters, only a potential to be, and out of this potential, in the flicker of eternity, came something—a thought, an idea—and then there were two things: the infinite sea of possibilities and the idea. And the idea was "I am." "I am" in the instant of its creation was the sea of all possibilities; yet in that instant, it froze in that form, becoming something quite different—separate and limited to that which it was at the moment it was conceived.

While the sea would continue to change, "I am" would remain eternally what it was in that moment: the truth, yet not the Truth, for Truth is infinite and infinitely changing, and "I am" could not change, was forever locked into the patterns existent at its birth.

"I am" looked at the sea of all possibilities and saw that it was separate—alone and lost. And in that time, within that moment of loss—an instant in cosmic nontime, an eternity in ours—is all the pain and suffering of the world brought into being. But the sea, gazing upon its creation, loved it, thus "I am" saw that it was not alone. Though eternally separate, it was also eternally bound to that great sea by bonds of love.

And the sea, being what it was, became that which it felt. It became Love; everything it became henceforth would be conceived in love, colored by love, contained in love. Love would be its law, its boundary, its limit. And from Love would flow the universe, time, space, the stars, the earth, mathematics, art, all of life, the Goddess, and the God.

"I am" loved its mother, the sea of all possibilities, and the sea loved its child/self in return, thus becoming Love itself. Between the two a bond existed—invisible, incorporeal, non-existent—yet completely there, and this bond connected them. Thus as one moved, they both moved, as one felt, they both felt, as one dreamed, they both dreamed, and as one danced, they both danced. This bond was Love.

From the One came forth the two, and from the two, came forth Love, in both its forms as noun and verb, being and becoming: Love, the body, and love, the act. Thus the spiral begins. Love is born in the rift between the one and other, and Love is the act that heals that rift.

This motion, this movement of borning and dying, of wounding and healing, of giving and taking, of knowing and forgetting, of going forth and coming back, is the stuff of life itself, the cosmic pulse in which, and by which, we exist—the heartbeat of the universe.

One . . . two . . . one . . . two . . . one . . . two . . .

In the great primordial sea of all possibilities from which all things come, there is no sex—no gender. *It* is neither male nor female. It just is. Once otherness existed, however, all opposites were born. Out of the one comes the two: the male and the female, matter and energy, life and death, good and evil, negative and positive, Goddess and God. And the tension between the two, the motion inward and outward—Love—is the invisible bond that supports the cosmos.

The power of Love is that it is both the opposite itself and the joining of opposites. It is both the object and the connection between objects. The face of Love is twofold, but its heart is one. Follow the pulse of Love along the lines of connection, and find the sea of all possibilities, the one Truth that is the source of all that is.

It was Love that gave birth to time and space, and Love that opened the door to death. It was Love itself, born in that conceptual sea, that created all-that-is. Love whispered and time began; Love cried out and space opened up; Love dreamed and the stars burst into brilliance; Love sighed and the earth bloomed. Love is the force that creates the universe. The bridge between timeless awareness and momentary joy, Love is the essence of what and who we are. For somehow, despite our limitations, we know Love.

Poets and artists, thinkers and healers, dreamers and actors, workers and players, each of us feels the rhythm and participates in the dance: one . . . two . . . one . . . two . . . one . . . two . . . . In every opposition is that primordial pair—oneness and duality—and in every joining of opposites is Truth. For Truth is the sea of all possibilities, beyond time and space, in which no opposites exist. Truth is the heart of Love, and whenever two become one, however briefly, Truth is.

Truth dreamed itself and birthed Love, and from Love, a universe. We dream of love and birth ourselves. We fall in love, think of love, make love, are love, give love, take love, refuse love, bask in someone's love; and out of all this loving, we create the form and substance of our lives. Love is the union of God and Goddess, giving substance and creating order in all-that-is. When we reach into ourselves, beyond the twofold face of Love, and into its heart, when we follow the connections to completion, we can know the sea of all possibilities and fashion our lives from it.

This conceptual moment lives in every aspect of our being, eternally spinning out the universe. Around it is built all our relationships, our politics—meaning relationships of power—all our potential. This moment is at the heart of all-that-is, repeated over and over again in different guise. It is the structural moment of life, the motion that joins space and time, matter and energy. Repeated again and again in an intricate web of relationships, this concept supports the cosmos. The structure of the universe is therefore, relational, not physical. It is a movement back and forth, to and from, in and out, and whether we look at a war, a rock, a love affair, or the relationship between mother and child, at its heart we will find this intelligence, this knowledge that continually creates the universe.

THE FIRST SPIRAL

God and Goddess

The Authors

The sea of all possibilities is the Goddess—Love itself—mother of creation, cosmic womb. Out of her is all life born. Systems, organization, natural law, and the authority these wield over us—these are the faces of the God.[1]

If the female principle is the sea of all possibility[2], the male is the imposition of order upon these flickering waters. As "I am" froze into form at the moment of its

---

[1] This may sound sexist, but it isn't. In future chapters I will show that we are all both male and female in mind if not body.

[2] Deepok Chopra calls it a "field of all possibilities," but I needed a metaphor that was bigger and wider in all dimensions.

conception, so does the God freeze the flowing waters of Truth into the known and knowable corridors of natural law. As the sea of all possibilities became Love at the moment it felt love, so does Love become all-that-is. As God and Goddess become one, forever joined in the whirling dance that binds them, so does the cosmos celebrate its existence in time. Thus is everything connected; thus are all forms bonded one to the other.

The Goddess

Thirty thousand years ago, there was only the Goddess, and she was loved and feared by all who knew her. She was the earth, the rain, the earthquake, and the thunderstorm. She was the sun, and all the clouds that covered her face. She was the blessed stars that shed some light on even the darkest night. The Goddess was the moon, keeping time upon earth; she was the seasons and the reason the earth would bear the fruits of survival. She was change, constant change, constantly unpredictable. And she was constancy as well, for the sun rose every morning, the seasons turned without fail, and the animals gave birth in the spring. She was woman. She was the Great Mother of all creation.

Ancient societies worshipped her and left behind them the signs of her religions—the spiral, the snake, the ax, pregnant and fertile figurines by the hundreds. She was the Goddess, Great Mother of all, and as she was venerated in Neolithic times, so were the women who led their people in worship of her.[3]

The Great Mother was both loved and feared, for who could know her? She brought forth the bounty of

---

[3] Woman in Sexist Society: Studies in Power and Powerlessness. Eds: Gornick and Moran. *Women in Other Cultures*, Ruby R. Leavitt. Basic Books: New York 1971.

the earth in spring and took it all away in winter. She gave us children and took away our mothers. She gave us pleasure in each other and moments of joy, yet could end it all at once, in the heartbeat of an earthquake or storm. There was no way to know her, only to pray for her to be generous with us, to give her a share in every hunt, and to care for the women and children, for these were closest to her.

Her priestesses were mothers. Her lovers were men. Man could know the Goddess only through woman. Sex was sacred, a form of worship through which the Great Mother could be known, the earth could be calmed, and the hunt could be blessed. Men would make love to the Goddess through her priestesses to ensure fertility and a plentiful harvest.

Woman worked the earth with her digging stick and hoe and brought food to the table. Woman birthed babies and brought new life into the world. Woman was powerful, creative, the earthly incarnation of the Mother herself—Great Mother Goddess—All-that-is. Her children asked her to explain why the sky was so high, and why only women had babies, and why the moon hid its face each month, and this is the story she told:

> One day, the Goddess looked upon herself and saw that she was alone. She had never known she was alone before. But having thought it, she saw that it was true. Before long, she decided to create a universe out of herself and to populate it with people, and birds, and animals. She would love and nurture these little creatures, and as she conceived this idea, she became pregnant, her belly swelled, and in due time, she brought forth all the universe: the sun, the moon, the stars and all the world and its creatures in the gushing waters of her womb. She set the sky above the earth to hide her face from the little

creatures below; she made the moon to keep the time so the people could measure their seasons, the stars to light the night, and she made women to have babies and men to care for them.

Of course, this is only part of the story. In time it came to pass that other tribes with far different beliefs, moving southward to feed their flocks, encountered these mother-loving societies and changed them forever.

The God

Neolithic societies spread from Asia across the continent of Europe as far as the British Isles, and as far back as 30,000 years ago. Many stories existed to explain our beginnings, as many as there were tribes. The Great Goddess had many names: Inanna, Nut, Ishtar, Astarte, Gaia, Isis, Mah; and she was worshipped in as many different ways. Each tribe evolved different myths to explain their ways as well as their place in the world, and when one culture came in contact with another and intermarried, myths changed to fit the new order. [4]

Coming from a harsher climate, male dominated tribes had begun to subdue the earth with the domestication of animals and agriculture on a large scale, made possible by the plow. These were not hunter-gatherer tribes, but tribes of cattle, goat, and sheepherders who used the earth and did not worship it. Having learned from the animals they tended that the male had first to deposit the seed within her before the female could give birth, they no longer believed that woman was the creator of life. She had become merely a vessel in which the male seed could grow. As she became, so did the earth.

---

[4] Campbell, Joseph and Bill Moyers. The Power of Myth. Broadway Books: New York 1988.

Spirals: The Connection

They used the plow to cultivate the earth, and because it was heavy, only men could do the plowing. Thus women in these societies were reduced to liabilities whose only asset was their ability to serve as wombs in which to grow the seeds of life planted by men. Men planted and harvested the grain. Men tended the animals and brought milk and meat to the table. And women prepared the food and served the men.[5] These tribes did not worship the Great Mother. Their God was male. He created the world. He created man and woman to serve him.

When little children asked how the world began, this is the story the men told:

> In the beginning, God created the heaven and the earth. And God said let the earth bring forth the living creatures. And God said let us make men in our image after our likeness and let them have dominion over all living things. And God created men and women in his own image. And God blessed them and gave them dominion over the earth and every living thing upon it. God said I have given you every herb and tree. To you it shall be for food, and to every living creature, wherein there is a living soul, I have given every green herb for food . . . .[6]

When these patriarchal tribes—who believed that the earth was theirs to subdue, and that God was male—

---

[5] *Woman in Sexist Society: Studies in Power and Powerlessness.* Eds: Gornick and Moran. *Women in Other Cultures*, Ruby R. Leavitt. Basic Books: New York 1971.

[6] It's interesting to note that this quote from the Book of Genesis tells us that every living creature has a soul that we should respect by eating vegetation, not meat.

came in contact with Mother worshipping cultures, the clash in ideologies could only result in war, and many fought for the Great Mother and shed their blood upon her body. The patriarchies won the battles. They had superior weapons, they had superior numbers, and they thought they had a superior idea.

They took to them the women and children of the conquered peoples, enslaving them. For even those who were chosen to become wives often became slaves in this new order; no longer were they the embodiment of the eternal feminine, no longer the incarnation of the blessed Mother. Under these patriarchal systems, they were vessels of male seed and servants of their husbands and masters. Their Great Mother Goddess was scorned as evil, debased, corrupt, debauched, low and sordid, and they were forbidden, on pain of death, to worship her. Those who did so anyway were called witches and were hunted down, tortured and killed.

Still, though men can control the bodies of others, they cannot always control their minds and certainly not their hearts, and many men and women, mother-lovers all, found ways to synthesize their cosmology with that of the new gods. Myths changed and numerous stories were generated out of the clash of these two ideologies.

It was said that the Great Mother had given birth to a son, who chopped her body to bits and made the heavens and the earth out of it. It was said that the Great Goddess had been split in two by the male deity and her body used to make the world and the sky. It was said that the Goddess had a son and slept with him to create a whole pantheon of gods and goddesses to rule the affairs of men. An idea would take hold and whole generations would follow it until a new idea was created, for religion is a living thing, evolving with the people who create it. And as people spread out and journeyed for the, they took their ideas with them and brought them into new lands.[7]

Because the patriarchal idea was eventually written down and enforced without mercy, it ultimately became the most dominant religion on the planet. As it mercilessly attempted to wipe out all traces of the feminine principle, it ruthlessly destroyed whole cultures, some as recently as yesterday—many African societies and Native Americans deprived of their lands and way of life by invading Europeans were matriarchies.

Yet despite the power of patriarchy, despite the weaponry and the ruthlessness, the female deity has survived. The Goddess still reigns as the Mother of Christ and is still worshipped as the Holy Virgin. Though she has been sanitized, is no longer the Goddess of sex and death, she has not been annihilated. She still lives in the hearts and minds of every woman, even those who don't realize it, and in many men. Today, women who worship the Goddess are no longer burned as witches—except in movies and perhaps in less enlightened countries—and we are watching a slow resurgence of belief as we once again acknowledge her power.

Union of Goddess and God

The Goddess and the God are just another turn on the spiral of time and space—a reiteration of the moment of awareness and all that happened and is happening in that instant of awakening. They are represented in stories with such power that they shape our very lives. At the center of the story of Goddess and God is the sea of all possibilities, the heart of love, and "I am" or con-

---

[7] Campbell, Joseph and Bill Moyers. The Power of Myth. Broadway Books: New York 1988.

sciousness. One . . . two . . . One . . . two . . . One . . . two . . . The reality at the center of the myth is in the dance, and the Goddess and the God are but instamatic photos of an event that is eternally unfolding. Today, because we know that male and female must meet to create life, we would make a new myth to tell our children, to explain their place in the world and the meaning of their lives:

In the beginning there was nothing, only an infinite, changing sea. It was not a sea of water but a sea of possibilities. Anything could happen within it. Then something did happen. An idea lit the sea and the idea was "I exist," and the idea separated from the sea and became a spirit hovering over the waters. For as soon as it thought "I exist" it could no longer be the sea of all possibilities. It was no longer anything-at-all, but had become something. Thus God was born. Now God looked upon the waters of the infinite sea and saw that he was alone. And cried out in pain. And his mother, the sea, heard his cry and let him play with her substance, creating all the universe, the stars, the heavens, and all the creatures of the earth out of her being, so he wouldn't be lonely anymore. And God stopped crying and saw that his mother loved him and felt love for his mother.

Now in that timeless instant of Godly despair and redemption, all humans were born and died and all religions grew up and were annihilated. But God loved his mother, the infinite sea of all possibilities, who in her love for God let him create the universe out of herself, and thus the universe, and all that is in it, is made out of that infinite sea of love, undying, everlasting.

And when God knew love and was no longer alone, hope was created, and all the beauty of heaven, and humans were given a soul and a heart that could know love, and a means to reach beyond their tiny existence and into the core of the infinite. And in our time, we call that means the Christ, the Buddha, or the tao, which means "the way." Though the details of religions differ, Truth is One, and union with all-that-is, through the relationship between Goddess and God, along the lines of Love, is the world without end that we seek.

And God and the Mother of God held hands and began to dance, a whirling whirlpool dance, spiraling ever and ever outward, and everything created out of the body of the mother was part of that dance. Every creature and event upon the earth takes part in that dance every moment of every day. The dance is the dance of life, and we all participate in it. It holds us together; its bonds are indivisible, infinitely complex and, just as infinitely, simple.

As the planets circle around the sun, and the earth spins at 1000 miles an hour; as water falls from the sky and is evaporated up to the mountaintops to fall once more upon us; as the tree bears seed and grows a new tree to bear seed; as electrons spin around their nuclei, so does everything in the universe and upon the earth, circle around and around and around—oppositions in balance. And that, my children, is why you like to spin, and why we all are dizzy down here. God and his mother, the Great Goddess, dance forever, in infinite whirling spirals in time.

First Spiral: God and Goddess
Dramatic Connection: Authors
Chakra: Root
Core Lesson: Truth

This dance, this structural moment happened at the beginning of time, is happening now, and will continue to take place until the end of time. The dance is life; it is order out of chaos. It exists. We cannot control it. We cannot use it. But we can understand it as the foundation, the truth upon which everything else is built.

THE SECOND SPIRAL

Life and Death

The Stage

Love. If the cosmos is built upon spider strands, a webwork of love, why do we have so much trouble loving? Why are we beset with loneliness and fear? If it is a cosmic dance and we are participants, why do we make war, and pursue pain? Why is it so hard to stay together? Why is life so difficult?

If you've ever been to a water park, you've probably taken the tube ride. Individual rides vary. Some take us to the bottom very quickly, so that we can stand on line and do it again. Some just go around and around in a kind of endless loop, and some of them—perhaps they're poorly designed—take us down from pool to pool, and in each pool we spin around and around, caught in a whirlpool. Getting to the waterfall that will carry us down to the next level takes work.

We half-swim, half-throw ourselves into the "fast lane" where the water is flowing quickly, and push off the sides and off other travelers. Most of the time we end up going backward, caught in the vortex, and have no choice but to try again. When we do succeed and splash down to the next level, it's only to do it over again. If we do it enough, the whole process becomes a kind of whirlpool in itself—get on line, go up the hill, go down the waterfalls, get on line, go up the hill, go down the waterfalls, and around and around and around.

Some people like this tube ride, though it does take effort. These people laugh all the way down. As in life, there are moments of frustration and cameraderie, times of realizing our work has been wasted and times of joy and completion. When everything comes together just right, we slip over that delicious edge and onto the next level of challenge. Despite these rewards, many find this ride too difficult. They'd rather be swept along by the current and quickly reach the ground. They want the water to do the work for them.

The best and the most exciting way to take this ride—and the hardest—is holding onto someone you love. A child is best, because children never give up. If it's hard making it from fall to fall on this ride by yourself, it's five times harder connected to someone else. However, you will laugh more.

The story of life is the whirlpool. We're all caught in it. We all travel round and round, trying to make some sense out of our lives, bouncing off others, getting stuck in a rut and suddenly finding the flow moving us onward. Some of us respond by rising to the challenge, taking the constant demands and changes in stride, and others by complaining that there's something wrong with the ride, that it's too hard.

We can get off this tube ride if we don't like it, but when it comes to life, it's best to grab hold of our rafts and go at if for all we're worth.

Riding the River of Time

Time for us is a river, taking us from here to hereafter, and it isn't always a smooth ride. Most of us find ourselves trapped in eddies that keep us swirling uselessly in place, or caught in a current that carries us in what we think is the wrong direction. Sometimes we hit the rapids; if we're lucky we don't crack our heads on the rocks, but sometimes we do.

All along this raging river, we work to attain that which we think will make our lives—that is, the ride—smoother. Some of us gather up riches, thinking this will make us happier; some of us try to do some good in the world, thinking this will make the world happier; some of us try to hold onto God, thinking that even if this ride is miserable, at least we'll gain heaven at the end; and some of us reach out for and try to hold onto love, thinking to laugh all the way down the river.

Sometimes we find a rock and climb out of the water. We build a home there, safe from the treacherous currents and whirlpools. We gather our family to us and hold on for all we're worth, fighting and even killing anyone who would threaten our security. The trouble is that there is nothing in life that can protect us from living. No matter how high we build our walls, or how carefully we plan our agendas, life cannot be denied. And life is in the river; the joy of life is in letting the river carry us where we are destined to go, even when this means struggling against it to get there. While we can take a break, climb up on shore and sun ourselves for awhile, we cannot stay there and refuse to get back into the water.

Often, we try to do just that. It's hard; we're tired; we don't want to swim anymore. We surround ourselves with material possessions and quality lifestyles; we plan our futures. Then we get sick, are betrayed, or lose someone dear to us, and we find that the rock is an illusion. The river is the reality. The river is life. We cannot avoid it. We can only accept, in passionate embrace, the uncertainty and turbulence. We can only truly live when we are in the water. We can only fulfill our destiny when we let the river carry us toward it.

The river is the dance, the sea of all possibilities, the Goddess and the God, the love of the universe out of which we are created. The river is our lives; it is us. Not just this small lifetime of which we are aware, but that endless life that flows eternally forth from the womb of our Mother. Just as the earth recycles the waters of its rivers into the sky and up to the mountaintops and down once again into the rivers, just as this cycle, this whirlpool, changes the nature of water endlessly from fresh river water, to salty ocean water, to rain, to snow, to ice, to river water once again and around and around; just so, do we exist, whirlpools within whirlpools, spirals within spirals, endlessly traveling through incarnation after incarnation.

Caught in an eddy of flesh in this moment, we lose track of the river, of the sky, of the cycle of change, and think that this particular spiral is all there is, when in truth, it's just a moment in time, a small whirlpool in which we're momentarily caught.

Love is fun—it's exciting, and passionate, and sometimes it's even sacred—but traveling down the river holding onto someone else is very, very difficult. We may be caught in different eddies, one going forward, one going backward; we hold each other back; we strain our muscles and our hearts trying to hang on. When we can't do it anymore, we let go, and then struggle against the current so that we can grab onto our beloved once more. We laugh, cry, scream, and rage against heaven, but no matter how much it hurts, love is a great ride. We take it because of the joy, and if we truly love, we never regret the pain.

Destination: Compassion

If we only went the way of love because of the joy, surely there would be fewer casualties floating down the river. We would stay with our beloved, live in passionate abandon, and die without pain. But joy is not the only reason for love. We must love, for it is through love that we grow. Love teaches us, for it's out of passion—which means, literally, to suffer—that we learn compassion—to suffer with. And out of compassion that we find the road between self and other, the sacred way uniting one heart to another. Through compassion we learn everything we need to know. Through compassion we know the Goddess and the God, and each other.

Compassion is, on this arm of the spiral, the connection between one and other, the nexus of the whirling dance of creation. Only through compassion can we reach into the sea of all possibilities and create our lives upon this plane. Only through compassion can we truly live. Through compassion we can know ourselves, each other, Christ, God, and finally, the Mother herself. For in compassion, we know that all things are One, and that the suffering of one is the suffering of all.

Compassion is not an easy lesson; it may take a thousand lifetimes and tremendous pain to learn it. Although we sometimes get little glimpses of what compassion really means, if we're still here, we still have work to do.

A few years ago, when I was discussing possibly adopting two children who had been abandoned, a friend of mine said, "Just remember, no good deed goes unpunished," and that, I realized, is often true. These children had suffered and could make me suffer. The reason a good deed, like taking someone in when they're needy, can bring pain instead of joy, is because we still have not learned our lesson. We think we have compassion—that's why we do the good deed—but we often find that we still have much to learn.

It is our mission to learn compassion, thus we are constantly tested in all our relationships. Because failure is painful we learn to tread lightly, demand little, and remember why we're here. Unable to bear the agony we know will come with it, we can, and often do deny love. However, refusing to do our lessons only puts them off for another day, another lifetime, creating future suffering for our future self. This is what we call karma—all the schoolwork we refused to do this time around, put off until the next.

Our classroom is the world, our teachers are each other, and the lesson is all the many faces of love. In every lifetime we learn a little bit more about it, study it from another viewpoint. Mother, father, lover, brother, sister, child, friend, giver, taker, student, teacher, scientist, artist, traveler, shut-in, victim, victor—we see it from all angles and slowly, over lifetime after lifetime, develop our spirit of compassion and grow toward perfection. We learn when to give and when to take, how to be open and still maintain our sense of self. We learn proportion, balance, and perspective.

We are students of the art of loving, for the universe is love, and whether we look at art, science, mathematics, play, or each other—we will find in love, the design, the relational context, that gives life meaning.

We do this because, while we are in some respects separate, at the heart of all that is, we are one. We are ourselves, but in a very real sense, we are the one, the divine itself. Divinity is perfect. Therefore, we must leave the perceptions of this little life behind and become perfect in our hearts, realizing that we are the incarnation of Love itself.

The dance of love on this arm of the spiral is no different than the sacred dance of life at the center: one . . . two . . . one . . . two . . . one . . . two . . . spinning ever outward. The key is in learning to step gracefully in the patterns of the dance.

Death?

There is no end to life, just as there is, in Truth, no beginning. While it appears to us that the river goes on from here to there, and ends in the ocean, it's only our limited perspective that prevents us from seeing that the ocean and the river are one and the same, that the water droplets that make up the clouds, and the water drawn from deep in the earth are all the same water. As is the water that circulates in our bloodstream and the water that fills our cells, and the water that the plant draws up into the fruit. These waters are cycled constantly from one form to another.

Life is like that water, connected to everything, permeating all that is. The universe itself is alive, inspired by the dance, animated by the Love at the center of creation. How can a universe that pulses with life, that creates incessantly, that exists so totally both within us and without; how can that be anything but alive? If we are alive, so must it be.

We breathe in air, supposedly non-living, and with it we create the energy and proteins of life. Where do we draw the line between life and non-life? When does oxygen that is non-living in air start living? Some would say that this happens when it is incorporated into organic molecules. The moment it's taken up by the blood, attached to an atom of iron, it is no longer inorganic O_2 but organic O_2. But did it change? Isn't it still an atom of oxygen? Is there any real difference between an atom of oxygen inside the body and an atom of oxygen outside the body?

What about the two atoms of oxygen inside the body that attach themselves to a carbon molecule and become carbon dioxide? The body doesn't need carbon dioxide, so it breathes it out. When does this molecule cease to be living matter? Or do we simply turn dead to living and living to dead as a matter of course? It makes no sense to draw any distinction between atoms inside the body and atoms outside it.

If we are alive, so is everything around us, because we are open systems, accessible to everything around us. It's all alive. If it doesn't look as if it's alive, think past this moment. In just a little while, a year or a hundred years, the paper you hold in your hands will have been returned to the earth and air, where atoms that now make up paper will one day make up the body of some animal, perhaps even a human being. The line between life and so-called non-life is only a matter of perception. With a wider view we can see that there is nothing that is not alive.

The universe is the body of the Goddess exalted by the God. It is intelligent. It thinks. It knows. It creates. And we are part of it. Like raindrops, we imagine we are separate but we are each of us, part of the water that is life. When we die, the flesh itself dissolves into its components and is re-used by the living organism that is the earth, and that part of us which is not flesh goes back to the sea of all possibilities to be born again.

Spirals: The Connection

My mother died recently and I have had a hard time reconciling myself to her death. I miss her; I miss her every single moment of every single day. I want her to read this book. I want her opinion ten times a day. But when I miss her the most, I think of two experiences. One was hers; the other is mine.

When my mother was a little girl, she was raised by a stepmother because her mother had died in childbirth. She never knew her mother and was never told that Adelaide wasn't her mother. What she did know, was that her mother didn't like her. Her mother was brutal and abusive. She beat her with wooden clothes hangers and locked her out in the snow. Every night, my mother went to bed crying and incapable of understanding what she had done wrong; why her mother didn't love her.

One night, when she was five, she had a dream. In the dream she was in a hall with three arches at the end and pews of worshippers. A woman came through the center archway and took her on her lap and held her and loved her and said to her, "I'm your mother, and I love you," and, for the first time in her short life, my mother felt safe.

Months later, at an aunt's house, she was going through a box of odds and ends, and she came across a picture. She looked at it and said, "This is my mother." Her father and her aunt tried to deny it, but in the face of her stubborn refusal to listen, they relented and admitted that her mother had died and Adelaide, the stepmother, was not her mother.

When my mother first told me this story, I was just a child. Yet it meant so much to her, I could actually see it as she told it to me. She wrote a story about it, and lit candles trying to draw the spirit of her mother. Her mother never came again, that I know of, but that once lasted her a lifetime.

When my mother died I felt as if the bottom had dropped out of the world, and I would fall and fall forever. I went to sleep crying and woke crying. I saw her die over and over and over again. Then five days after her funeral, I had a dream. I left my body and flew across a meadow to a university where my mother lay on a stretcher in the hall.

She was still bruised and hurt from her long illness, but I could see that she was much better. She was younger. She saw me and sat up and said, "Oh Debby, isn't it wonderful? I'm going to marry Eph!" I was worried about my father and said I wouldn't tell him, though it didn't seem to matter to her. In fact, when I asked about him, she said that that was over. We talked briefly, then she had to go behind a wall where I couldn't follow. Finally, I flew back over the meadow, started to fall over the road, felt my cheek touch the road, which was soft, and opened my eyes, my head on the pillow. I was happy.

Eph was an old friend of my mother's, a musician and an intellectual whom she had always admired. He and she (along with my father and Eph's wife) had worked on a play together when I was twelve, and I think those were among the most fulfilling days of her life. When she told me she would marry Eph—whom I hadn't thought of in ten years—I was very happy for her. I knew her next incarnation would give her a lot of what she'd missed in this one. It made sense. It was right.

When I woke up from this dream that wasn't really a dream, I was quite happy. I had remembered something important, which I'd forgotten in the emotional tailspin following her death. For many years, I had been in love with a man who was always picking up and going somewhere. Sometimes he'd disappear for three or four weeks, and I'd never have a clue where to reach him. At the time, I was so obsessed with him, I couldn't bear our separations, and when I didn't hear from him for a long time, I would leave my body during sleep and go and find him.

Without fail, if I found him, I would hear from him the next day or the day after that. I taught myself how to leave my body in sleep because I needed to be near him. When my mother died and I needed to be near her, I automatically went out of my body and found her.

I spoke with her many times in the months after her death. The last time, I flew through space and found her on a stage in a kind of theatre with people all around. I understood that she was working through the issues of her past life, but I only cared about my own need to be with her. I called out to her, "Mommy!" and she looked at me in confusion. Someone told me I shouldn't stay, that it wasn't good for her, and I immediately found myself back in my bed.

But I was not satisfied. I had to see her, so I went back. This time she was in the same theatre, only she was now in a bed. My uncle Benson, also deceased, came up behind me and whispered in my ear that I couldn't stay. Again, I was sent back to my body.

Still, I was not satisfied, and I flew once more to this place. This time I was met outside the door by two genderless beings who explained that I was doing my mother no good, causing her to regress instead of move forward. The words they said appeared on their foreheads so I would understand and remember. And I did. Still, I had to see for myself and went one last time into the theatre. Now my mother was in a hospital bed and had an IV in her arm. This I understood. I went back to my body and knew I would never seek her out again. In fact, I saw her again only once.

I had a dream in which she was getting all dressed up, putting pearls in her hair. I said, "Why are you getting dressed up, Mommy?" And she answered, "I'm waiting for your father."

Two days later, my father died.

There are other instances I could relate but these are the nearest to me, and because of these experiences I know, not just intellectually but truly from my heart, that life goes on. The spirit continues on, a seed from which to bring forth a new body and a new life. No different in its own way from the seed that buries itself in the earth and one day becomes a rose.

Nothing in life has an ending, everything changes form and changes form again. Seeds become flowers, flowers become fruit, fruit becomes seeds; fall becomes winter and winter becomes spring; oceans become clouds and clouds become rivers and rivers run into oceans; dust to dust, ashes to ashes and back again. Everything continues in endless, spinning spirals in time.

Rebirth

We are intimately connected to the source of all creation—the sea of all possibilities—and when we die to this life, we go back to that sea and create a new one. My mother used to despair of this because she wanted to keep her memories. She wanted to keep her *self* intact. Happily, despite her worries, in a way, that's what she did.

When I leave my body in sleep, I am me. There is an essential part of me that is me no matter whether I have a body or not. This is my soul, my spirit. During this lifetime I have accumulated knowledge and information. At my death, the information will be forgotten, but the knowledge will remain. In my next incarnation, I will take that knowledge with me as part of my personality. Though I won't remember details, it will still be me.

Spirals: The Connection

Anyone who has ever watched more than one baby grow from infancy will have noticed that each baby is different. Each baby is born with a personality, a way of relating to the world, a kind of inborn knowledge. For instance, one of my babies was very serene. She was an observer. She watched me, my husband, and each of her toys with dispassionate joy.

When she was two, I asked her if she was writing a book—she was always looking into things and trying to figure them out. She spoke of herself in the third person: "Joanna is going to eat." She had no particular skill with people and let me know at six years old that her younger sister's inborn ability to wind people around her exquisite little finger, was quite a mystery to her. One child was born knowing how to charm people, the other with a burning curiosity to know and understand how it all works. What makes them different?

There are those who will say it's in the genes, it's nature; others will say that somehow I taught it to them; it's nurture—perhaps the difference occurs as early as pregnancy. Still others will say it's a combination of both genetics and environment. I believe it's a combination of three factors—nature, nurture, and spirit.

A child is born with a spirit, a personality, a particular way of looking at and dealing with the world. Into its life comes a parent, or two, who responds to that child in terms of who that child is. For instance, if a child is charming, the parent may be more tolerant than if it's not, and this will influence the child's perception of itself and of the world around it.

Besides reacting to the child's personality, the adults in its environment will attempt to influence it in various ways. Attempts will be made to train the child, to "civilize" it, to instruct it in cultural matters. This is environmental influence. It goes on throughout life. We learn, we assimilate what we've learned, and we grow and change according to what we've learned.

Appearance is largely genetic, but if you look carefully you'll see that it changes. One day a baby looks like its mother, a week later like its grandfather. A child can be born beautiful and grow ugly, or ugly and grow beautiful. Appearance draws on genetics but is not limited by it. If we perceive ourselves to be beautiful, that is, if the spirit and genes we're born with meet with the approval of those in our environment, we will be beautiful. If not, our appearance will suffer along with everything else about us.

We are spirits immersed in matter. We create that matter to suit our personalities and cause ourselves to be born to parents who will help us achieve our spiritual goals. If we are born to parents who are uncaring, selfish and even brutal, we may wonder how this can be true. How could we have chosen to be born into such a situation? How could we have chosen to be hurt?

If life is about learning to love, then perhaps the answer is that we needed these parents in order to make progress. When we step into our lives we bring with us a set of assumptions. In fact, our lives are classroom assignments: follow these assumptions to their logical conclusions.

For instance, our brutal parents might be a lesson in compassion, and learning to understand and forgive them might be our purpose this time around. Or we might have left our former life having lived selfishly. Realizing that we should have been kinder to people, we would be given the opportunity to follow that assumption to its conclusion in this life. We might have parents who are cruel so that we would understand how it feels when people are unkind. In fact, we would probably encounter unkindness everywhere we go until we learn to *be* kind even to those who are cruel, at which time, our lesson learned, we could go on to other lessons. There's always something to learn, and life will ever be ready to serve up another exercise.

The Role of Coincidence

I once taught a public speaking class at a university and I was intrigued when one of my students made a speech regarding her belief in Jesus and proving it by the coincidences that had happened in her life. She didn't call them coincidences however; she called them answers to prayers. She had been late for her graduation and had prayed for help and when she arrived, fifteen minutes late, the ceremony had been, to her mind, miraculously held up.

I thought it fascinating, because through coincidences like this, she had become a "born again" Christian, intolerant of any other belief. Yet, I, too, had experienced amazing coincidences that proved to me the intelligence of the universe. I hadn't become born again, at least not in the Christian sense, and I had never lost my respect for any individual's right to choose his or her own way.

The only differences I could find between us were in exposure and tolerance. I was exposed to spiritual ideas in wide variety from a young age and actively sought new ideas as soon as I was able. This young lady had only been exposed to one spiritual idea and was taught that it was the only right idea. Thus, when she experienced those miraculous coincidences that happen to all of us, she interpreted them to mean that Christ had answered her prayers.

When such incidents happen to me, and they occur all the time, I interpret them to mean that I am in touch with the living Intelligence that inspires all of life, as are we all, and that somehow I have touched it and created some good in my life.

It's harder to take responsibility for the bad things that happen to us. Why wasn't I born rich? Why did my father never love me? Why is one born beautiful and another ugly? Why should some have everything and others have nothing? It isn't fair!

It isn't fair. The system is out of balance; the rich get richer and the poor get poorer; the middle class grows smaller. The earth is being depleted; the environment debased. People are starving and dying at this very moment in order to support the rich and varied lifestyles of the industrial nations.

Most of us don't even realize how dependent we are on the resources of poorer countries, or that people work for slave wages and live in unspeakable poverty in other nations in order to supply us with the endless consumer products we are taught to require.

Nevertheless, in spite of, or perhaps because of, the essential unfairness of the system, we must take responsibility for ourselves because that is our only hope of changing our circumstances and our lives. Perhaps it isn't fair. It's difficult to reconcile the fact of children being born with AIDS with any standard of justice, but if we can think that there is some justice to it, some underlying reason, we can be empowered. If we can think that our lives are in some respect up to us, we can take charge of ourselves and find a way to make a difference.

If we think, "The system stinks and I'll never get what I need because I can't change the system," we make ourselves into victims, unable to alter the course of our lives. On the other hand, we don't have to think "Oh, I must have been bad in another life, look at what's happening to me in this one." This is as self-defeating as the first idea.

Spirals: The Connection

Instead, we can find the balance point and say, "I must want to grow in some particular knowledge in this life. That's why I have all these challenges to face. I'll work through them and through myself, and discover my purpose on this plane." The first way of looking at it puts us outside the system, unable to affect it (except perhaps violently), the second enslaves us, and the third sets us free. The difference between victim and victor is simply a matter of viewpoint.

We are all in touch with spirit; it is the core of our being, and we can see it at work in everything we observe, but perhaps never more clearly than when we study the coincidences that have danced through our lives, protecting us here, saving us there, turning up in unexpected places to make our lives better, even for just a moment. Coincidence alerts us to the truth lurking beneath the confusion. "There is order and reason here," it whispers. "Take another look." For instance, several years ago, after I had quit a teaching job I was tired of, I went out to dinner with a friend. I hadn't decided what I was going to do, other than substitute-teach if necessary, but in the back of my mind was the realization that I'd rather write.

The food was terrible and my friend thought she should tell the waitress. It turned out the waitress was just helping out the owner of the restaurant. In fact, she was working on creating a food criticism magazine and was looking for writers. I wasn't even looking for a job, but the universe knew I needed the extra work and there it was, handed to me. At least, that's what I thought at the time. The truth, however, is that that particular job didn't pan out. I interviewed some powerful local people, and wrote an article, but the magazine never opened and I never got paid. I could say that my time was wasted, but I don't. Instead, I look at the incident and see what I learned from it. I did want to write! I enjoyed the process. It was a worthwhile lesson.

Sometimes, when you're on the right road and are fulfilling your destiny, coincidence begins to work in a more powerful and obvious way. This is because the coincidences that happen at this stage of awareness are not really coincidences. They are, in fact, manifestations that you create. For example, I did become a writer, and I was able to support myself and my children through my work. But I wasn't publishing my books; I was working as a freelance writer doing mostly technical and commercial work. I was still a long way from where I wanted to be. Then the recession in the late nineties that put so many dot.coms out of business lost me most of my clients.

I saw this as a chance to do something different and decided to publish my books, this one first. One thing led to another, and because I had to support my kids and I was always thinking of paying the bills, I began my own POD publishing company that took off in a big way.[8] This was because my company was created to help writers and would-be writers be successful. It wasn't created to exploit writers as so many other POD publishers were doing.

After a year or so, I discovered a basic problem with POD was that no returns were possible. In the publishing world, returns are a fact of life and booksellers can return any book, but not, at that time, POD books. I was deeply distressed by this and started thinking about a solution. A couple months later the solution came knocking at my door: a company was being set up to

---

[8] Llumina Press: www.llumina.com

take POD returns and wanted mine to be the first company to work with them.

Not every coincidence works the way we might want it to, but these particular ones and many others like them, have convinced me that all is well with the world; the universe is intelligent and full of love.

There is nothing to fear, for death is an illusion, as ephemeral as that rock we believe we rest upon, or our very flesh itself, which too will pass away in time. The river, however, is real, carrying us ever forward toward the sea of all possibilities from which we were born and to which we must return. The river is Life—all of life—a spinning vortex pulling into the center even as it forcefully spins out, a never-ending spiral taking us from sea to clouds to snow covered mountaintop, to stream to valley to pool of clear water, to muddy banks, to cool wells, to domesticated ice cubes, to wild rapids, to raging waterfall. Like water, Life changes form but it never ceases to exist.

Second Spiral: Life and Death
Dramatic Connection: The Stage
Chakra: Sexual
Core Lesson: Courage

We are thrust upon this stage at birth and must play out our roles. If we try to hide, afraid to live fully in our own story, we will only have to do our lessons over in another lifetime. So take courage. Death is an illusion and there really is "nothing to fear but fear itself."

THE THIRD SPIRAL

Men and Women

The Actors

Men and women are different. Students of human nature have argued the whys and wherefores of this observation for thousands of years, and scholars, today, believe that differences between the sexes may be biological, environmental, or even a bit of both. However, after all is said and done, it's most likely that gender differences are cultural.[9] Boys and girls, even in the same household, are raised differently, and men and women grow up belonging to different cultures.

---

[9] There are many books on this: I recommend Deborah Tannen's *You Just Don't Understand*.

Though boys and girls may grow up in the same neighborhoods, even in the same houses, they live in different worlds. Boys play in groups with a leader who tells the others what to do. Boys' games have winners and losers and many rules. Boys often boast of their skill at something and argue who is the best.

Girls, on the other hand, usually play in small groups or in pairs. They take turns at their activities, or play games (like 'house' and 'school') that have no winners and losers. There is also a difference in boys' versus girls' conversational styles. Girls say "Why don't we do this," or "Let's do that." Girls who issue commands, or who are overly assertive, are considered "bossy."[10]

In the world in which boys grow up, status is always an issue—one is either above or below another, being told what to do, or telling others what to do. Girls, while not unaware of status, are more concerned with being liked, with fostering intimacy in their relationships. Girls and women generally form networks where everyone is on the same level, not hierarchies, where one is above or below someone else.

These two cultures meet head on whenever a man and a woman fall in love. Despite the relationship, a man is still a man, and still concerned with whether he is one up or one down in relation to the other, and the woman is concerned with whether or not the intimacy is there.

For men, intimacy often means doing things together, yet for a woman, it usually means talking about feelings. Thus relations between men and women frequently break down as we try to understand each other across this cultural divide, a gap we neither recognize

---

[10] Statistically, this is what the research has found. However, there are always exceptions.

nor comprehend. This is especially so in romantic situations.

Male vs. Female Culture

The origins of female culture go back over 30,000 years. When Goddess worshipping cultures met God worshipping cultures, the result was not the assimilation of one into the other. Instead, female culture hid itself within patriarchal systems—passed on from mother to daughter—and continued to exist through thousands of years. Though women have been abused by men over thousands of years of enslavement, they did not lose their identity. Slavery, after all, does not necessarily annihilate a culture. It may just send it deep into hiding where it waits for freer air in which to breathe.

Though the Israelites were enslaved by the Egyptians, they never forgot their past or their beliefs, and Jews the world over still celebrate their release from bondage every year at Passover. Today's African-Americans are more aware of their history than any generation has been since slaves were freed in North America at the end of the Civil War. As it becomes possible for a people to exist without persecution, they become more themselves. Thus it is for women.

Though we endured thousands of years of enslavement to the male ideal, nevertheless, whether in our genes, in the memory of our mothers' touch, or in the stories we share, we somehow have retained all our latent femaleness, and it is emerging in what is now called female culture. In Western cultures today, women have more power to explore themselves than they've had in millenia. The spiritual side of women, locked in stasis by a power wielding, death-dealing patriarchy has exploded into being in this new age.

Women are different from men. While male culture establishes hierarchies—this is higher in status than that—female culture establishes networks. Women create connections on a level field—relationships between equals. This significant difference between male and female[11] reflects the basic nature of the universe. The female principle is the sea of all possibilities, the mother of creation, wherein everything is one, and the male principle is the establishment of order, or hierarchies and classifications, upon those waters. Between them is love.

This does not mean that either male or female is superior to the other, for the facts are:

1) Ideas of superiority are largely masculine.
2) We are, each of us, both male and female.

As we have a mother and a father, and as we have inherited physical traits from each, so too have we inherited the male and female ways of knowing. Our differences result from the way we are raised, and the cultures we are raised in.

In other words, we are capable of both male and female understanding, but we are often limited by our

---

[11] This difference stems from the differing roles of men and women in the creation of life. Because woman gives birth, she knows who her progeny are. She can see her future in the eyes of her children and knows that she lives on in them. And it works the other way too through mother to grandmother all the way back to the first stirrings of life on this planet. Men, on the other hand, do not know who their progeny are. While they can create laws against adultery, create institutions that limit woman's ability to co-habit with more than one man, give their names to their sons, the fact is, without DNA testing, it's often impossible for a man to know if his children are really his. That makes it harder for him to know that he will live on through them. That's why he's driven to succeed in his own right, and why he creates social systems and hierarchies.

knowledge of the world and of our place in it. We have the potential to be either male or female, or to be both, regardless of our anatomy.

Dancing Together

This third spiral pulls men and women into the dance of life. For, in every way, we embody the same principles that exist at the center. We are a physical incarnation of the act of creation, that which took place between our mothers and fathers, and that which takes place, at this moment and every moment, at the center of time and everywhere.

Though we are both male and female in mind and soul, our bodies are usually[12] one or the other, and the act of love in bringing together the male and female—or "I am" and the sea of all possibilities—recreates that moment of universal conception which lies at the heart of time and space. Sex is the coupling of Goddess and God repeated in human form, and in performing the act which creates life, we recreate ourselves.

Thus sex is sacred, reiterating the beginning of time and consciousness and the birth of God. The act of love is the material form of the vital relationship between one and other which ignites the stars and supports the heavens. It is both our undoing and our only hope.

As the sea of all possibilities and "I am" create love so do we, and it is out of this substance that we are made. The love that draws us to each other is iden-

---

[12] There are people born with organs of both sexes.

tical to the love that holds each of us together. We are the sea of all possibilities and we are the children of that sea, "I am." We are love itself and we are the bonds between the two aspects of ourselves. We are both one and two. We are right and left brained, holistic and sequential. The right brain, the holistic side, is the sea of all possibilities, and the left brain, the sequential side, is "I am," the ego. We contain both within ourselves and we are one.

As expressions of the very center of creation, it's no wonder that we get confused when we fall in love. It takes us a whole childhood and adolescence, possibly a whole lifetime, to integrate the parts of ourselves into one. Now try and integrate another into that creation; it's no easy task.

Love is the joining of separate individuals into one, the fitting together of a puzzle of infinite dimensions, because as many as there are facets of you, as many aspects as there are to you—physically, mentally, emotionally, and spiritually—there are reflections in the mind, body and soul of the one you love.

This is the dilemma we all face. How to gaze upon, become entwined with, go into and hold within ourselves, infinity itself and somehow maintain a sense of self, defined and limited in many of the ways we were before we fell in love. Yet, as we succeed in integrating who we are into who our loved one is without losing ourselves, we grow. As we create bonds between ourselves and others, we become greater. Love, however painful, is necessary, for without it we cannot grow.

Mapping the Steps of the Dance

Growth is a difficult process, requiring both endurance and commitment. As we outgrow one stage of development we need to be able to move on to the next with a minimum of discomfort. Nature provides for this by making it possible for us to create inner charts of our progress by which we can navigate. In order to make sense of ourselves within the world, at a very young age, we create the first of these blueprints, or maps, to which we can add as more information comes in.

This map is an open circle, a spiral. At its core is one central belief or assumption around which we organize other, related beliefs as we acquire them. A child's original map is probably organized around its mother as the center. As we mature, our map gets more sophisticated, and it's the alteration of this map that is so painful in growing up.

As long as new information doesn't affect our central beliefs we can absorb it without discomfort. One day, however, something new comes into our lives—another human being, an event we perceive to be a failure, a problem we can't solve—and our blueprint suddenly requires enormous reorganization.

The new information does not jibe with the core assumption upon which we base our persona and out of which we've built stories about who we are. It becomes necessary then, to undergo a kind of disintegration; we feel confused; we're lost; we don't know what we feel. We struggle through these emotions and, eventually, put the map back together again, including or rejecting this new knowledge. We are reintegrated. A new story has been created.

This is one of the reasons drugs are so dangerous for young people to take. Instead of going through the growth process—disintegration is painful, after all—people take drugs to feel better. They do feel better, at least momentarily, but the drugs stunt their growth and they remain emotionally immature. Until they are willing to endure the pain of disintegration, reorganize their inner map, and reintegrate around a more mature belief system, they can grow old, but they cannot grow up.[13]

Sometimes, especially when we lose someone we love, this disintegrating process goes all the way to our very core and we think we just might die of it, but what really happens is that we are forced to redesign our core beliefs. For example, the map I used most of my life was organized around the core belief that love between a man and a woman was all that mattered. Around that were arranged such concepts as self sacrifice for the relationship, and the man comes before my family. In fact, at the center of my map was not me, but him. Then I got divorced. My core belief was annihilated. The center of my life was gone. I was a failure. I had chosen the wrong man to place on the throne of my heart, and was probably incapable of choosing the right one.

Though it took several years of painful growth, I finally did reintegrate around a stronger center. My core belief now is that I am here to learn and to teach, to give everything I can to the world and to the people around me. At the core of my map is not a man, but the universe and all the world, my belief that I can make a difference, that in some small way, I matter. At the core of my map is, not the egotistical "me," but the universal "me," the "me" that recognizes its connections to all that is. I'm comfortable with this, as well as completely certain that it will not last. Sooner or later, I will be called on once again, as we all are, to redesign my central beliefs.

---

[13] This has nothing to do with drugs used as sacred, vision-enhancing vehicles of enlightenment. It is the overuse of drugs for recreation without preparation and spiritual purpose that is life-destroying.

There are those who are so fearful of this mental and emotional disintegration that they never allow it to happen. Instead of examining themselves and learning from their lives, they put their faith in authorities outside who tell them what to believe. This is what fundamentalists (of all faiths) are all about. Refusing the responsibility inherent in self-awareness and exploration, they accept that other humans can know more than they do about who they are and how they should live. And because their fear of self-knowledge, and all the responsibilities it entails, is so great, they will even accept death (with promises of heaven, of course) rather than dare to change their core beliefs.

Disillusionment and disintegration are necessary acts upon the path of growth. Although it is exquisitely painful to re-map our core beliefs, it is also incredibly valuable. The phoenix that rises out of the ashes of self, the newly integrated individual, is certain to be the best we've ever been. And it is love—thorny, painful, awe-inspiring, beautiful love—that drives us toward our own perfection.

And on and on . . .

Men and women, dancing the dance of creation, rise up in emotional spirals to expanded levels of consciousness, joining ourselves first to one person and then to others and finally to all of creation. Growing in wisdom and compassion over the course of many lifetimes, we explore the natural boundaries of love on this plane and go beyond them, to explore the same structure of relationship on other planes. At the center of creation is a relationship that, repeated over and over, on every level of the universe, is Life. Love is our means to understanding it.

Third Spiral: Men and Women
Dramatic Connection: The Actors
Chakra: Solar plexus
Core Lesson: Trust

Love can be painful, but without it we cannot grow. Our teachers are those who love us, for it's in relationships of love that we learn to trust ourselves, each other, and Love itself.

THE FOURTH SPIRAL

Power and Love

The Conflict

Some say power, or authority, comes from God. Others that it comes from the people and is granted to the political or religious authority. Still others say that authority is personal, that we should each follow the beat of our own drum. Most of us fall somewhere in the middle, believing that we have exactly as much personal authority as God and the economic order will allow—that is, after we've done what we have to, we can do what we want.

I believe, however, that power comes from inside. Each of us draws our life force from a source of power within us—our soul. Though this is not really a separate part of us, we can think of it that way for a moment. We might think of the soul as a conduit, a pipeline through which the power at the center of the universe, the power at the moment of creation, is directed to us. Through our souls we are in touch with the Goddess, the God, and the love that is them and which lies between them. Through our souls, we are one with the universe, we are connected to the source of all-that-is.

Like an invisible umbilical, our soul joins us to Love, the power that knits the cosmos and inspires us with life. But the soul is not a part of us, like another organ. It *is* us; it permeates each cell of our bodies, each atom of matter. Like the photon of light that, according to quantum physics, is both a particle and a wave, our souls are tiny links at the center of every atom that connect with the whole universe, as well as eddies in time that are uniquely us. In a way, we live, not just in the four dimensions of which we are aware, but in another, soul-dimension, where we can feel the connections between all-that-is and all that we are. Here we can feel the power that structures the universe.

This power begins in the vortex at the heart of each atom where the dance of Goddess and God reaches the physical plane. Here, where protons and electrons spin out webs of matter and relationship, the sea of all possibilities is molded by "I am," and intricate patterns in the dance become molecules of life.

It is intention and desire that drive the ellipses of electrons. Subatomic particles appear and disappear, seemingly dependent on whether or not they're being observed.[14] This is why, when we relate to something, when we focus our attention on it, we can change the very structure of our lives. This power to change the

---

[14] For a description of Quantum Physics without the math see Fritjof Capra's *The Turning Point* or *The Tao of Physics*.

"system" is the ability to form relationships—to focus awareness on something and connect to it.

We each have this power to relate and are capable of drawing more from the source. All our relationships, both within ourselves and with others, are formed out of the continual give and take of this power. It is constantly in motion, oscillating back and forth at every level. From negative to positive and back again, the exchange of power is so fast at the subatomic level, that we can only perceive it as a vibration. As long as it is in balance, as long as negative equals positive, the speed or frequency of the vibration remains high and we feel good.

At the visible level we can observe this exchange of power in action as we give power to those we love and accept it from them when they give it to us. Every time we make someone feel good about something, we give them power. We input a positive charge into the system. Every time we hurt someone, by becoming negative, we take power away. Even the smallest transaction, a greeting, can occasion the loss or gain of power, and on this level, even small things can upset the balance.

Power in Relationships

How does this exchange of power work? If I say to my daughter, "Do this," and she ignores me, I feel weak. After I've said it a few times and gotten no results, I feel powerless to affect her behavior. By ignoring me, she has negated my offer to relate and succeeded in taking my power. She feels powerful. Therefore, I might say to her, "Do this or else!" becoming even more negative than she, and pulling that power, and more, back again. Suppose my daughter still refuses to comply, and I resort to force? I am no longer weak; I am powerful.

However, she is crying and powerless. In this instance, I have taken power by pulling it forcibly from her, and done violence to our relationship. Having seized power without respect for the other individual, I have hurt both of us in the process.

In human beings, power is understood as emotion. When we are powerful, we feel happy, elated, and confident. We have faith in ourselves and in each other. When we're weak, we feel depressed and miserable. That's why it's so hard to feel positive when we're having problems. Negative emotions are caused by a loss of power, and when we feel negative we invite even greater losses.

Negativity can become a vicious cycle, spiraling down to deep depression and even illness. We get weaker and weaker unless we receive an input of energy from outside ourselves, or change our own emotional state by opening ourselves up to the source and giving away the power we draw from it.

Giving power functions to draw more power through us. When we give, when we establish a flow outward, more is pulled into us from the source. When we take, the flow is inward and power does not flow from the center into us. It's as if we are a tank with an inflow and an outflow. As long as water flows out the outflow, more water can flow in the inflow. When we pull water in through the outflow we can't get any new water through the inflow, because we're full. In simple terms, the more we give, the more we get.

Or, to look at it another way, every human being is like an electrical switching station, or a telephone switchboard, with thousands, perhaps millions, of invisible wires, like feelers, reaching out for connections. Where two positives—two admirations—meet, they cannot touch because like repels like. Yet they are positive, so the gap across which they reach for each other is

Spirals: The Connection

filled with power from the source. In fact, it is the source.

The charge is positive and the repulsion between them is negative. That gap, that "positive negativity," holds the relationship in balance in the same way that such gaps keep electrons spinning around protons and planets spinning around suns. That gap is the balance point, the heart of the dance, the relationship between the sea of all possibilities and "I am."

On the other hand, when two negatives meet, they repel each other, creating not a positive negativity, a balance point, but a negative negativity. That's why, when both partners in a relationship become negative, they each want to get away from the other as quickly as possible. There is no attraction across the gap.

Sometimes, we want to touch each other, however, not just admire each other across the gap, and one of us changes polarity along one or more lines, becoming negative to the other's positive, so that we can connect. Power flows here directly from one to the other. If one becomes too negative the balance is thrown off, however, and if we connect at too many points, leaving too few wires open for relationships outside this one important relationship, we begin to lose our capacity to relate to each other or to anyone else, sometimes even to ourselves.

The negative one tries to back off or hold back, or do whatever it takes to restore the balance, while the more positive partner tries to connect more lines for precisely the same reason—to restore the balance.

We cannot relate when we have collapsed into each other; the whole nature of relationship requires that there be two. The gap, the space between particles, and between individuals, is necessary to life. All of creation spirals around it. It is the relationship between God and Goddess; it is the feeling between "I am" and the sea of all possibilities; it is the structure of the universe; it is one and it is two; it is I and thou; it is Love. While we sometimes desire to bridge this gap above all else, we do so at our peril, and we'll see why shortly.

Negotiating Power

According to James Redfield of *Celestine Prophecy* fame, we humans compete for energy (or power) with each other and this competition is at the root of all our misery and heartbreak. This is true as far as it goes, as is Mr. Redfield's suggestion that we can learn to draw power from nature. Power, however, is everywhere. There is no shortage, and we can learn to draw it from wherever we are. We do not have to visit a virgin forest to expand our power. All we have to do is give generously, with an open heart.

Wherever we are, whomever we're with; whatever we're doing, it never hurts us to give power away—as long as we do it willingly and without reservation. It does hurt us to hold onto it, or to take it when the other does not want to part with it.

Power is what it's all about. From your relationships with your children, to the relationship between yourself and the government, to your relationships at work, power is the underlying dynamic. When you negotiate power with your friends it's probably over simple things—shall we do what you want or what I want? Shall we go to this movie or to that? As long as both parties remain positive and give willingly of their power, there is no problem.

Energy cycles back and forth without hindrance, enabling the vibrations at subatomic levels to maintain their speed. However, when someone becomes negative, pulling power from the other along the lines of relationship, the energy vibrations slow down, descending into lower and lower frequencies, resulting in feelings of anger, sadness, and depression.

Our first experience of power begins in infancy. Though relationships between parents and children begin with the parent in the position of authority and the child subordinate, babies begin to negotiate for power almost immediately by crying when they need attention, and by giving attention in the form of smiles: smiles or whines, positive or negative. [15]

By the time they're toddlers, babies are experienced veterans taking their struggle for power to new heights. The terrible twos are illustrative: by saying "no!" the child is also saying, "I am." No longer willing to comply with the wishes of the parent, this negative is designed to usurp the parent's power. The awareness of self creates this conscious need for power. For what am I, if I can do nothing with what I am? I exist only so long as I own control of my own body and mind, and only so long as I am separate from the rest of all that is.

This is the paradox that lies at the center of all our turmoil. We wish to be together, but we dare not melt the boundaries between us. Just as "I am" at the center of creation can never again be the sea of all possibilities, we cannot be ourselves and be the other. Instead, we negotiate power, and balanced in the center of this give and take, we find ourselves, both separate and unique, and one with the whole of life.

It takes a certain amount of trust in each other to maintain this balance between the positive and the negative, and without it all our relationships are thrown out of kilter. For example, some people come to awareness as children finding so much resistance to their autonomy—their self-direction—that they must pull further

---

[15] Some parents put their children in a position of power from the moment they're born.

and further away from the center in order to maintain their sense of self. Imagine a two year old boy who is threatened and abused whenever he does something wrong. His parent's consistent violence over his choices drives him to distrust himself, to feel anger at his parent and at himself, to fear that he will never be able to make right decisions, and that he will never be worthy of love. He has, in fact, lost a great deal of power.

Instead of finding a balance between the two sides of self and between self and other, and understanding at the deepest levels of his being the connectedness of all life, he is cut off, out of step with his parents, the world, and a part of himself as well. Unable to see the wholeness of life, he cannot give, therefore he cannot draw power through the gap. Such children rarely manage a give and take with authority, cannot consent to being governed, and instead find themselves in a battle for control of their own lives. They cannot get power from the source so they must get it from other people.

This power struggle can absorb entire lifetimes. The boy will grow, not into healthy relationships where love is given freely, but into relationships where power is always an issue to be struggled over. He will fight to maintain his separateness in any relationship, and may never know what it feels like to be one with another, except for the brief experience of sexual joining. He may never know the joy of surrender. Needing to maintain his walls, he will intentionally take power from relationships but will not readily give it back.

Power Dynamics

Power cycles back and forth constantly in all our relationships, and it is the transaction of power that makes us happy or unhappy with other people. Think

Spirals: The Connection

of the river. If both partners in a relationship are traveling down the river holding onto each other, they are constantly encouraging and supporting each other. "Grab that guy!" "Pull yourself along the shore!" "Hold onto me; don't let go!"

If one does all the work and the other just holds on without giving any support or making any effort, the relationship is going to suffer. The energy level that supports the relationship—the frequency—will go down. Eventually, the relationship—those two arms reaching out for each other—will fall apart for lack of an attraction across the gap. It becomes work to give.

We could look at power relationships in any area of life to better understand these dynamics, but when we look at people in love we can see very clearly how all relationships work. While we may not like to think so, power is the stuff of 'love' itself. Being in love makes us feel as if we're floating on air because we've generated and infused a great deal of power between us. If both partners become unwilling to give (power) to each other, the relationship will end in divorce.

When individuals interact, there are only three ways they can deal with power—they can give it, they can hold it back, or they can take it from each other. Holding back is essentially a technique for taking power, which psychologists call passive-aggressive behavior and it is negative, so we will, for the moment, call it taking.

When all is said and done, there are just three ways that power transactions can take place:

1. Both give power (+ +)
2. One gives and the other takes (+ -)
3. Both take (- -)

There are thus three ways to transact power—one is completely positive, one is both negative and positive, and one is completely negative. We should note that because we are talking about trillions of infinitesimal, microscopic exchanges, at the visible, macro level, positive and negative are on a continuum, and events can go slowly from positive becoming more and more negative as more and more connections are made, and vice versa.

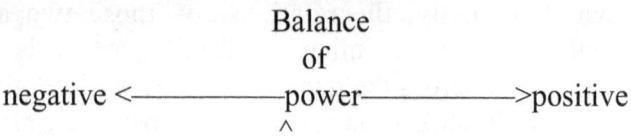

Love and power are one, and when we admire someone, we willingly give them the gift of power. If admiration is mutual, we begin to share the power within us, each growing stronger as a result. We say we are in love; we feel happier, more confident, ready to take on the world. We are, for the moment, more powerful, more beautiful, more lovable, and more loving than we were before.

When we fall in love, we feel lighter, not because our burdens, or the weight of our bodies have changed, but because we suddenly have more strength to carry ourselves. Our vibrational energy has increased; we resonate at a higher frequency than before. Power, when it flows freely between individuals, also flows freely from the center creating a double loop (resembling the symbol for infinity or the strange attractor of chaos theory), which empowers each of us, making us surer, more confident, and more aware.

We pull more from the center, give even more, pull in more from the center and from each other, and so on, around and around and around, in this case, spiraling up and filling us with joy.

Although we are passionately enjoying the thrill of love, we want even more. We want not just to admire each other across the gap, but to touch, to actually become one, to close the gap, and it is at precisely this point that things can, and often do, go wrong. As sexual beings, the need to touch overrides the need of individuals to maintain the separation, and slowly, inexorably, we are sucked into the maelstrom, connecting one line of self after another, until bit by bit, we begin to lose our individual power and our ability to relate as independent human beings.

In and of itself, there is nothing wrong with this. We are designed to do this because it works in the maintenance of the human species. It is not unusual for a mother to sacrifice herself for her child or for men and women to sacrifice themselves for their passion (which is supposed to produce children). We are made like that. Thus we marry and, if we are lucky, become less and less like individuals and more and more like one being. As long as neither partner becomes too negative or too positive, as long as a balance is maintained, it can work.

Problems occur when we feel love for someone and experience that undeniable need to connect across the gap, but are unable, for one reason or another, to do so without reservation. We may be emotionally unavailable. Unable to draw power from the source, we are unable to give it. Or we may be physically unavailable, being involved with someone else. In either case, crossing the gap, for even the briefest moment for even the most delicate of touches, can result in disaster.

All those little switching points we mentioned earlier become, in such relationships, sexual attraction. After connecting one after another, there is nothing else we can do but connect the larger systems themselves, the bodies, along the lines of relationship.

Then something goes wrong. Some little trust betrayed, some careless opinion that hurts us in a secret place we haven't even revealed, and we begin to hold back. Though still giving, we're not quite so certain we can give it all, and what we receive, we keep for ourselves. Our partner, who may not even know what has caused us to hold back, may continue to give, until he or she begins to feel that the flow of energy is not making the complete circuit. This person then begins to hold back a little as well, becoming just a bit negative, and the first, feeling the lessening of flow, holds back even more.

Give and Take Relationships

While empowering love almost always exists at the beginning of intimate relationships, it often gets lost somewhere along the way. Many relationships are held together simply because the two people involved remember the love that their mutual admiration inspired in the beginning. For the sake of the past, they stay together, hoping to rekindle the flame. However, when the power flow changes, becoming one sided and off balance as one becomes negative and the other positive, the loop collapses, and the flame begins to die.

This leads us to the situation where one person gives power and the other takes it. In this case, no energy is generated, and nothing is drawn through the gap. Some relationships are born like this—when someone tries to buy another, for instance—and many relationships that start with empowerment descend into this state. Sometimes one is the taker and the other the giver. Then they may get angry and switch roles. Either way, the relationship is off balance.

Interestingly, takers in these relationships often think that they're giving. Consider Jane. She's in love with Jerry, and she can't understand why Jerry doesn't want to spend as much time with her as she wants to spend with him. She feels she's willing to give her whole self, but Jerry is only prepared to give part of himself. Jane discusses this with Jerry, but nothing changes. Jerry feels that Jane is not giving, but trying to *take* all his attention. He needs *more* space after she initiates a discussion on this subject than he needed before.

At times, Jane has nothing to give—she's already given whatever she had—and what she's now missing she wants to get back from Jerry. She believes that she can only get that power in a love relationship, and therefore she'll do anything she can to get it circulating again. Not wanting Jerry to get angry and pull further away, she hides her attempt to take power by calling it giving. She wants more of his time; she wants more of him, so she offers herself.

Jerry refuses to receive what is offered—Jane's whole self—because it feels like she's taking something from him. Though he too may want the flow of power to be in motion again, he doesn't comprehend his part in the problem. Jerry suggests that Jane is too aggressive and wants too much. The more she wants from him the more he retreats, holding back because he fears that she will take too much and leave him with nothing. All Jane's protestations of love and desire to be closer feed Jerry's ego. He takes in the power given and keeps it for himself.

Jerry, we might argue, is just protecting himself from Jane's aggression. By putting up a wall, however, by protecting himself, he's actually attempting to keep himself outside the relationship. By not allowing power to flow, he is able to take Jane's aggressive offers of love in, and feed off them. His taking is not aggressive; it's passive, but it's there nonetheless.

By holding back, Jerry gets to keep the power from the relationship and gain a little more every time Jane tries to make him open up by giving more of herself. If he's careful, he can probably maintain this situation for years, gradually depleting Jane's resources. He will be strong and Jane will be needy. He will be powerful and Jane will be weak.

However, it's only Jerry's ego that is strong, not Jerry's soul, and therein lies the problem. In this case, Jerry has given up on love, not because he didn't trust the other, but because he didn't trust Love. Unwilling to place his life in the hands of another and afraid to lose the power that sustains him, he sacrifices the relationship in favor of his ego. It's far safer to hold onto what he has than it is to risk it all for something he neither knows nor understands.

Jane's attempts to take are also twisted around. Instead of saying "give me," she says, "I give you . . . ." She's afraid of losing, so she conceals her attempts to take power, and sacrifices her ego. She believes that power comes, not from the other, but from the relationship, and she's willing to give everything to make the relationship work. She, therefore, gives more and more in her attempts to restart the power flow and risks coming up empty.

Believing that power can only come from love, Jane doesn't realize that it can flow in any relationship. She can recharge herself in her work, in her friends, in her children, in a painting, a hobby, in meditation, in nature, or in any creative act, as long as she gives wholeheartedly to it. The problem is that all her wires are connected to Jerry, and before she can connect to anything or anyone else, she has to re-establish the gap between them.

Because the relationship is off balance, each party swings one way and then the other, like a pendulum. The loop grows large on one side and small on the other, then deflates on the large side and inflates on the small.

When each participant begins pulling power from each other instead of from the source, thus choking off the influx of real power, the open spiral of their love closes down. Without the Love of the universe pouring through the gap, powering the relationship, all that remains is a struggle to grab the power left circulating in the loop, power that is destined to degrade to lower and lower frequencies, leaving both partners unhappy, distressed, and alone.

The funny thing about finding power in everything we do, is that it is not a selfish act. In order to take from the source, all we need do is give. It doesn't matter in the least where we give, or to whom. All that matters is that our attitude be positive; that we give wherever we can, reckoning neither the cost nor the payback. When all we do is give, the universe conspires to give back.

On the other hand, when we hold onto power gained from a relationship and do not release that power somewhere else, we lose doubly. First, because we are stuck now in our own little world unable to renew ourselves in the source, and second, because the energy we've taken, the energy which now belongs to us, cannot stay at its high level unless it is kept in motion. This energy begins to degrade, to drop into lower and lower frequencies. We don't feel good, and we may become ill. When we get our power by taking it from others we find that we never have enough.

Two Takers

The situation where one holds back and the other takes without subterfuge can be quite unpleasant. When

Jerry holds back, Jane eventually gets so angry that she lashes out at him, threatening to leave, trying to force him to give back the power he has taken. While holding back is a neat tactic for extracting power from the other with little risk of discovery, and taking, under the guise of giving, can sometimes gain temporary ground, all out taking of power without deception is tantamount to a declaration of war.

If Jerry is afraid of losing Jane completely, when she confronts him he may open up a little, giving up some, but not all of the power he has taken. Polarities switch momentarily as Jane takes and Jerry gives. Or, something else might happen. When Jane comes out in the open, declaring her position, Jerry might not back down. He may come out in the open too. From holding back to outright taking is a very short step, and a declaration of war on the other's part can end in both becoming takers.

When both people take in a relationship, each tries to hold onto what they have and get some more back from the other. Neither is able to draw from the source because we can only do that when we are positive, when we let our power flow out from us, pulling more through the gap as it does so. Clenched up and unable to give, Jerry and Jane find themselves in the midst of a full-blown, declared power struggle, which in intimate relationships, frequently ends in divorce or separation.

Faces to the Wall

When givers and takers reach the ends of their ropes, when they have tried everything they can to make their relationship work, when they have given everything there is to give and it's not enough, when everything has been said and done, when love cannot be reclaimed and all hope is gone then both partners hold back, turning away from each other, exchanging nothing. In this case there is simply nothing left to say. The individuals are finished with each other; they cannot give anything more. There still may be power to be negotiated, but it will always result in a fight. It's only when enough connections have been severed, and both partners have begun to get power elsewhere, that they may begin to be able to talk.

There is no way to get involved in discussions about human relations without getting involved in matters of power. We spend most of our lives negotiating for power in one way or another. Whether we're teenagers trying to talk our parents into a later curfew or adults trying to talk our boss into a raise or ourselves into a new job, we are going to be dealing with power. And, when it comes to power between two people there are only these three ways to negotiate.

So What Can We Do?

Part of the new age philosophy includes the win-win situation, or, I should say, the win-win situation is a reflection of the new age. We are beginning to see that taking power is not the way to go. While previous generations, especially of men, may have been taught to take what they wanted from the world, today we look for empowerment, we strive to build networks rather than hierarchies, and in our most intimate relationships we're learning that we must ever be open, for to hold back is to commit our love to a lingering death.

There is a doctrine of biological science that states that "ontogeny recapitulates philogeny." It means that the human fetus goes through all the stages of human evolution in its growth from a one celled creature to a baby. For a while it looks like a fish, for a while a reptile. In our relationships, there are stages we go through as well.

Few relationships stay at the empowerment stage, but most go through it and it's glorious for as long as it lasts. Most of us, eventually, settle into a comfortable truce, wherein each knows how much they can expect to get from the other and gives back just the same amount. Stasis is maintained. If they are not passionately happy, the partners are not passionately unhappy either. Power flows—not a river, perhaps, but a rivulet—and is cycled back and forth between the two. Balance is maintained.

Some people, and I was one of them, are not satisfied with this stage. They want to be wrapped up in the flow of power, to drown in the whirlpool. We call this romance. When it starts to fade away, we may fight to maintain it, even when what's standing in our way is our partner. Those "women who love too much" are, like Jane, trying to get the flow back in motion, fighting against the man they love because he is feeding his ego instead of the relationship.

In fact, such people, men and women alike, need to drown in the whirlpool, so that they can disintegrate and reintegrate around a more substantial core—for Jane, a core that includes the world and herself, not just her partner; for Jerry, his partner and the relationship, not just himself. Until that happens they become takers; they become givers, and back again, each in an attempt to reestablish the flow.

The stages of love take us, ideally, to a place where we can experience the joy of love, feel the flow of the river of power without losing our sense of self and our ability to act as individuals. Across the delicate balance of that positive negativity we can enjoy and appreciate each other without changing polarity and making so many connections that we are unable to function in other areas of our lives.

In a truly giving relationship, we would both offer our whole selves at the same time that we keep our whole selves apart. We would give it all— trusting absolutely in the generosity of the universe to replace anything we give away—and we would also take it all. In a truly giving relationship, we don't expect to get only from our partner. There's a whole world out there with which we can relate. We can share power in our work, with our friends, with our family, and give it back to the one we love as freely as he or she gives it to us. That way we both end up with more than we had when we began.

This may have been easier when our communities were small and we mattered not just within our families but in the world. It's harder today. Often we leave each other when the power struggle becomes conscious. Unable to bear the pain we're causing, any more than we can bear the pain we're feeling, we reach out for new relationships and, perhaps, start over at the beginning with someone new. That's why people marry a similar partner over and over again, and why one divorce tends to breed the next one. The problem in the relationship, that it involves taking rather than giving, does not go away because we change partners. Our lack of faith follows us wherever we go.

When we steal power in a relationship, we hurt those we take it from and ultimately, we hurt ourselves. Each of us requires power to become a fulfilled, self-actualized person. If we take a person's power and don't give it back, that person ends up unable to take care of his or her own needs, much less ours. And we lose as well, for what use is power, if it leaves us alone?

When love is dying, when we feel the flow of power drying up, our first instinct is to blame the other. It's their fault it's all gone wrong. However, it's more than likely that if we really look, we'll find at least part of the problem within ourselves. Are we giving what the other needs or are we giving because we want to take? Are we asking too much of our partner? Are we accepting what our partner is giving? Maybe we need to draw more power from our other relationships, from our work, from other things that make us happy, so we can give more genuinely to the relationship.

Sometimes it takes time alone, to work on ourselves, before we can work on a relationship. Before we can integrate ourselves into the life of another, we first have to be integrated. All the parts of ourselves have to be one. Before we can have a mature love, we first have to be mature. When we are at peace with ourselves and able to draw from the source within ourselves, centered on our purpose in life, then we are ready and able to love, knowing that there is no end to the flow of love as long as we are not afraid to give.

Fourth Spiral: Power and Love
Dramatic Connection: The Conflict
Chakra: Heart
Core Lesson: Generosity

When we are afraid, we cannot give without holding back some part of ourselves. But when we give generously—without fear—we get everything we want and need. There can be no power struggle if we do not try to take power. Rather, we accept all that life offers without fear, and it keeps providing us with power direct from the source.

THE FIFTH SPIRAL

Good and Evil

Motivation

Good and evil are probably the most difficult of all oppositions to reconcile because, in a very real sense, we live in the maelstrom created in the nexus of this spiral. Good and evil are the stuff of life on earth, the basis of most of our religions, the conflict in our drama, and the often hidden subject of many of our debates. We desire good and fear evil.

The book of Genesis says that we learned of good and evil when Eve ate the fruit of the Tree of Knowledge in the Garden of Eden and shared it with Adam. According to the story, they ate the fruit, saw that they were naked, and were afraid of God because of it.

But there's more to it than that. Although she feared that God would be angry, Eve desired the fruit. The serpent of the story is that niggling, wiggling desire worming its way into the parts of her that were able to take action.

Many religious traditions have interpreted this to mean that the fruit of this tree gave Adam and Eve knowledge of their sexuality: They saw they were naked and covered themselves. But let's look a little deeper.

Adam and Eve had been naked all the time, and it wasn't their nakedness that roused God's anger. It was their disobedience. God knew they had disobeyed when he saw them *clothed*. That they had become aware of their nakedness made it obvious. The fruit of the Tree of Knowledge granted that awareness. Or did it?

What if the fruit of the tree had no effect whatsoever? What if it was as innocent as a plum? Would we still be abiding in Eden? I don't think so. The fruit, after all, is a metaphor. No, it was the act of taking the fruit that made God angry. This act, which God had forbidden, suddenly became the focus of their lives and the focus of their awareness. Knowing they had done wrong, they became afraid of God, saw how small and weak they were, and covered themselves with fig leaves in an attempt to hide their sin (their wrongful act).

Thus fear was born. Fear is the fruit of the tree, and if God is all knowing and all powerful, then He forbade his children to eat of this tree on purpose because he knew they would, and in doing so, they would learn.

Plunging us into the vortex of this spiral and teaching us to fear, Genesis has been used for millennia to also teach us to be wary of what we desire. "Look," we've been told, "there will be consequences. Desire is the route to sin, so we cannot let desire rule us."

Out of this patriarchal story about what makes us human, we've come up with ideas like original sin. We've blamed women for listening to the "serpent," thus turning them into something soiled and evil. We've

Spirals: The Connection

created a Devil out of that same serpent that is able to make people do wrong. With this story to back us up, we claim other religions are wrong (evil) and justify everything from burning heretics to destroying whole civilizations.

This story of guilt, fear, and sin is at the root of all patriarchal religions. Based on this story, we are taught that we are born evil and must strive against desire. The free will granted us, in this interpretation of the story, is the freedom to walk away from what we want. But what if this interpretation is not exactly correct? What if there's more to it? What if we need to manage fear as much as we need to manage desire? What if there is no Devil, only God?

What if, by using this potent myth as the basis of religion, certain patriarchs were able to take power and use it to rule people?

Power is one of those terms that can generate whole libraries of books; however, for the purposes of this chapter, there are only two types: power over others and power to do things. Perhaps it is sometimes expedient, and may even be necessary, to seize power over others, but can it ever be right? Granting ourselves the power to seek what is right and good and to take action on our desire for these things is however, something else. That something is freedom.

We began this book with a story about the beginning in which the sea of all possibilities birthed "I am" out of itself, bringing, in this moment, all of creation into being. First, there was only the sea and a potential to be. Then, there was the instant of creation, separation, and then something else, "I am"—or awareness of self—existed. Let's examine that moment more closely. For in the instant of birth before the sea recognized and loved its creation, there was a nanosecond of terror as deep and wide as infinity: the terror of being alone, weak, and separate, the fear of death, the need to survive. This is the same fear that Adam and Eve felt when they realized they had been so bold as to disobey God. In that moment, they became (in their guilt) separate from the divine.

This moment is the one in which fear was born and out of fear all its children: prejudice, anger, hatred, *self*-hatred, cruelty, and war.

While this rift between the sea of all possibilities and "I am" was healed in boundless love as the relationship between them came to be in the next nanosecond; nevertheless, the echoes of that timeless moment of terror continue to ripple through the structure of our reality.

Rationalization

Good and evil, as we'll see, are not so hard to understand, but we muddy the waters endlessly because of our innate ability to rationalize, making what is simple complex.

No matter what we do, we almost always think we are doing what's right. Oh, we might be wrong once in a while, but evil? Of course not. We meant well, didn't we?

This starts very young. The first time a child hits his little brother or sister over the head with a truck and has to face his mother's anger, he begins learning to rationalize. "But Mommy," he cries, "I didn't *mean* it!"

We're so good at rationalizing that before long, we even believe it ourselves: Of course, I didn't mean to hurt her feelings. Of course, I didn't mean to fall in love with my best friend's boyfriend. Of course, I didn't mean to get drunk and crash the car. After enough years of this, some people get so good at it that they never recognize their responsibility for anything. "Hey," they say, "Don't you understand, I did it for the public good."

Or "If you'd only been nicer to me, I wouldn't be looking at other women."

Humans have this wonderful built-in way to keep themselves feeling good about themselves. It is probably a survival mechanism, because, after all, how can we be really effective at surviving if we're feeling like we're wrong and undeserving? Such feelings always spiral down into depression, and the more depressed we get, the less capable we are. So we rationalize.

We all start out wanting to be good. While a baby is born knowing only what it *wants*, it soon learns that it's wise to please its mother. It learns to smile, sleep through the night, sit up, use the potty, and babble. These are good behaviors; they make mother smile. However, at around two years old, most children figure out that mother is so enamored of them that they can get away with anything, so they decide to take a walk on the dark side. Suddenly, that all-powerful woman with absolute dominion over us, may begin to show her *own* dark side. If it's at all possible—without losing our sense of self—most of us choose, during this stage, to stay on the side of right.

Those who don't choose the "good" at around two or three years old may find themselves in a struggle against authority throughout their lives. It can happen for a variety of reasons: mother demands too much; we get more attention by being "bad;" it may even be that we like to tease her, and she doesn't get the joke. Whatever the reason, we still need to feel that we are good, so we begin to rationalize: she's wrong to get so mad; what's the big deal? She's stupid. She's jealous. That's when we start blaming our mother (and later the school, teachers, society, the world) for who we are. Not feeling good is a heavy burden for anyone to carry, especially a child.

Thus we all develop the ability to see events as if we *are* right, even when we're wrong. And because we're designed to see ourselves that way, we can only come to grips with our faults if we deliberately go looking for them, at which time, we tend to go overboard, taking on too *much* blame.

Some of us seesaw back and forth, seeing ourselves as right one day and wrong the next; some settle somewhere in the middle knowing they can be wrong (though they're probably right); and some go to the other extreme, always placing blame somewhere else. The fact is, because we rationalize as easily as we breathe, we frequently cannot look objectively at our own behavior. We're not even that good at clearly seeing others' behavior if it reflects on ours.

This is not to say that we *never* recognize our own wrongdoing. Sometimes, we know what we want to do is wrong. We know we should not do it, but we do it anyway. We may be torn apart internally, but when all is said and done, we knowingly do wrong, just as Adam and Eve did. The results of such actions usually are not pleasant. We suffer self-doubt and fear; we may hurt people we love; we may ruin our own lives. Evil is, after all, its own reward, and after a time, our ability to rationalize may have to jump in and save us from our misery: We didn't mean it; we had good reasons; someone else made us do it; it was the circumstances; we had no choice. All these rationalizations—excuses really—give us a little breathing room and allow us to survive.

Some religions allow for confession and penance to put guilt and shame away from us. This may be a good thing because most of us, especially when we're young and driven by desire, do things we know are wrong. If we don't belong to such a religion, then we take the consequences of our actions and have to, somehow, live with them. We might choose our own penance. Perhaps we look for something to do that is good, that will somehow make up for what we've done that is wrong.

I always thought it was funny how people, after going through the worst times of their lives, start thinking about giving something back to the world. I did it after getting divorced. But I see now, it's penance, and it's necessary.

If seeing ourselves as good helps us to survive, how can we trust our decisions? How do we choose between desire and fear? We don't know all the facts, and usually we can't know what will happen if we do or don't do what we want. Sometimes, all we have to work with is probability. The very idea of right and wrong, good and evil, is often irresolvable, so we look outside ourselves for answers, to people we place in authority: religious leaders, doctors, teachers, psychics, psychologists, government officials, and others.

When right and wrong elude us, we make laws laying out the rules of civilized behavior, and we try to follow them. Sometimes, however, our impulses and desires get in the way. For instance, let's say a man in a jealous rage, kills his wife. During the act, he doesn't care if it's right or wrong, and when it's over, he may be able to tell himself he had good reason: she was cheating on him; she was going to run off and take his money. These reasons allow him to live with himself and his act. It's only when the law catches up with him, and he is forced into a corner that he might admit to himself that he did wrong. And then he goes to jail, where, I've heard, everyone claims they're innocent.

Beauty and the Beast

Another face of good and evil is visual. American culture is permeated with ideas of beauty and ugliness that go right to the heart of our deepest fears. We worship beauty and youth, and shun that which we see as ugly.

Everything beautiful is good and everything that is not beautiful is bad. Our movies feature beautiful heroes and heroines, and villains that range from ugly in spirit to absolutely physically horrifying. When we are not happy we feel "ugly." When things go wrong, we feel there's something wrong with us. We love babies because they are beautiful. We fall in love with beauty, but it's a rare individual who will fall in love with the beast.

Beauty and ugliness, reflections of good and evil, are difficult to comprehend and transcend because they are the most personal, affecting us at primitive and instinctual levels. On the whole, we live our lives in the search for youth, hoping to avoid the pain, decrepitude, and failing senses that we believe are the inevitable result of aging. But there's more to beauty than youth and innocence and more to ugliness than aging and death.

Within each of us is Beauty: the one who is good and pleases others, the one who is giving and altruistic, the one who believes and has faith, the one who shares and is unafraid of what tomorrow will bring. But within each of us also dwells the Beast: the one who is afraid and insecure, who refuses to give, who takes power and uses it against others. The Beast is everything we wish to put away from us, but which despite our best efforts surfaces now and then in fits of temper, insecurity, and despair.

Remember the story of Dorian Grey? He kept a picture in his attic, which showed every evil intent or action he ever committed while his actual face and body remained as beautiful and innocent as a youth's. Dorian Grey had managed to separate the Beast from himself, so he was able to stay young and good-looking. But we can't really do that, and so every terrible, fearful or desperate act we undertake makes its mark upon our bodies.

It is this that we fear: that the lines of aging on our faces reveal our errors and our mistakes as surely as a map shows the world where to look for Disneyland, that the sagging muscles and spreading waistlines demonstrate our laziness and ineptitude, that the aches and pains of aging demonstrate our incapacities and failings. We know, unequivocally, that you can't tell a book by its cover, but that doesn't stop us from judging the book that is ourselves in terms of what it looks like. Although we can see the interior of the book, all the pain and glory written within, we know that others cannot, and we fear that they will judge us by the outside alone.

Unfortunately, it's true that many people do just that. And although we expect it of adolescents, we are not necessarily so mature that we don't ever do it ourselves—look at others and see only the surface. Because we do it, we know that others do it too. And that's what makes us want to hide the ugliness we know is within. The trouble is when we put up a mask to hide the ugliness, we also hide the beauty, because what is beauty but truth? What is beauty but authenticity?

To hide what we fear is within us, we cover ourselves up with a cloak of falseness that hides everything. And from that point on we live in a world without color where everything is muted: our feelings, our understanding, our connections to the world, and especially our ability to feel love and joy.

We are too fat; we are too short; too tall; our noses are too big; we're too old; our teeth too crooked. No one is one hundred percent happy with their appearance, even those whom our culture regards as the most beautiful. For instance, I have a daughter who is 5' 7" tall, weighs 110 pounds, measures 34-24-34, has a terrific sense of humor and great joy in life. She has huge brown eyes and blond hair and is what most of us would consider a knockout. But do you think she's happy with her looks? Of course not. Her hair is too curly, she has a pimple, her left pinky has a tiny scar. Give me a break! I tell her if she's got a problem, the rest of us should just drown ourselves. But what can you do? She believes that she's not perfect inside, and this is what she sees in the mirror. It's not her hair she's looking at; it's her spirit. Or, more to the point, it's what she believes is her spirit. It's her ego, her fear.

So it is with all of us. Because we see ourselves from the inside, we're sure that everyone can see how worthless we really are. And it doesn't matter in the least that we know, intellectually, that this is not so, that we all have faults—bits of the Beast—lurking within. As we judge others, so we judge ourselves.

It all comes down to belief, doesn't it? Because as we'll see, Truth encompasses all aspects of reality. There is no one Truth. We can as easily see ourselves as beautiful as we can see ourselves as horrible. We can study our faults and find the underlying passions of which they're constructed, and understand the incorruptible beauty of living that made us what we are in this moment. Or we can hide from that truth and claim its opposite-that we live in an imperfect world and are imperfect parts of that reality.

I keep thinking of the alien in the movie of the same name, the most horrifically ugly creature ever conceived as far as I'm concerned, and I keep coming back to this: someone created that creature and made it so ugly that it became beautiful to its creator. Beautiful in its completeness, its thoroughness, its perfect dedication to the ideal of ugliness. Someone loved that creation and owned it and worried that it was not good enough and added detail upon detail until it breathed ugliness like we breathe air.

From this perspective, beauty doesn't really have anything to do with appearance. It has to do with being finished, completed, faithful to an ideal, real, unmasked, vulnerable. It has to do with being singular, unique, owning up to our differences and being unafraid to show who we are.

Spirals: The Connection

Ugliness is quitting short of those qualities. It is stopping with half a smile instead of a whole one. It is hiding the self under masks of false behavior. It is being uncomfortable in our own bodies, unable to open ourselves up and be vulnerable. That's why babies are beautiful—their spirits are exposed. They hold nothing back. And it's also why many old people (not all, however) are ugly—from a lifetime of holding everything back.

When I was in the midst of a divorce, I had a dream. In it, I was in a house and the walls were covered with blood. Someone in that house wanted to kill me; I could hear him ranting in the other rooms. So I flew from the house and into the air, trying to get away as fast as I could and turned to see a great black monster following me.

Howling with anger, it pursued me as I flew across the sky and the world below me erupted into flame. I was terrified as it gained on me and thought I would die, and then I heard a small voice within me saying, "Even the devil needs love." I couldn't escape, so I turned and embraced the horror, pulling it toward me and kissing it. And then suddenly, I was on a quiet beach with the moon and stars overhead, and the "devil" had turned into a little boy. I held his hand and we were at peace.

For a long time, I didn't know what this dream meant. I thought the monster was my ex-husband. I painted a picture of it chasing me, and when he saw it, he even thought it was him. But I see now, that the Beast was part of me, the part that judged me and saw that I had failed, that I had failed miserably. And it wanted to kill me. By embracing it, I set myself on the road to healing.

One more story. I knew a man once who was the Chief of the Seminole Indians. I had been hired to create a video for a woman named Betty Mae Jumper. She was the tribal storyteller and the video was to recreate their ancient stories on tape. I thought Betty Mae was an incredibly unattractive woman. She must have weighed three hundred pounds and she was old. So when I was speaking to Chief Billy about the video and he said, "we must dress her in tribal dress so we can bring out her beauty," I was momentarily taken aback. Then I realized that he saw her with eyes of love, as the woman who had rescued him from death as a child, as a woman he'd grown up with and known forever. He could see her beauty where I could only see her fat. We're all beautiful to someone, and it has nothing to do with what we look like. It has to do with who we are. It has to do with relationship.

Beauty and ugliness are just physical reflections of beliefs held within the mind. We can make ourselves beautiful by what we believe, but others can perceive us as ugly because of what they believe, and vice versa. Beauty and ugliness are illusions, mirrors of our minds, reflections of desire and fear, of good and evil.

These opposites are really just another spiral on the structure of time and space, another turn on the wheel of life and death. Beauty and ugliness are just two ways of looking at the same exact thing. And they have to do with belief, with acceptance of what is and with judging what we see. When we see with our left-brain and ego only, we see only surfaces and we can perceive ugliness. But when we look with our complete selves we see that there is no such thing. We see that it's just what it is. It's with our egos and our fear that we judge. But if we go a step further and look with our hearts, we see that it's more than we imagined. It's beauty without end.

Cultural Definitions of Evil and Good

Defining the good is as difficult as defining evil, and our definitions of these states are largely dependent on who we are, what families we're born into. We all be-

Spirals: The Connection

long to different cultures. We are men, women, or children, each of which is a culture in itself with many subcultures. There are different rules of behavior for men and boys than for girls and women. There are different rules of behavior for children than for adults. These sets of behavioral norms, rules, and ideas define each of the cultures to which we belong, and we begin to learn them from the moment we're born. From day one, we learn the expectations of our family cultures, and when we grow up a little, we become part of others such as Boy Scouts or kids who work after school.

In America, because most of us come from somewhere else, we each start out with a different set of cultural expectations. Greek culture is different from Jewish culture, which is different from Irish culture, which is different from African American or Japanese culture, all of which are different from Native American culture.

In addition to gender and ethnic cultures, we each also belong to religious cultures, racial cultures, local cultures, even food and television cultures. The list is endless. When we think of all the groups we belong to, we begin to get an idea of how many different cultures are a part of our lives, pulling us this way one day and that way the next.

Each of these cultures has its own definitions of what is good and what is not. For instance, those who belong to a culture of naturalists would not think it much good to spend a day at a shopping mall, while those of us who are materialists think it the best sort of day. People who are into junk food do not think organic food tastes good and vice versa. At an Irish-Catholic wake there will be dancing and drinking, but a Protestant funeral will be more somber and subdued.

Culture is often invisible. We don't always see our cultural differences because we don't even know we belong to all these groups. For instance, I, an American, was married to a Greek. We had many differences of opinion about business. He believed it's a "dog-eat-dog" world and that it's permissible to do almost anything as long as you win. You can deceive people, cheat them, do anything it takes to win. Winning is smart, and everything else is irrelevant. Family and some friends are not to be treated like this, but everyone else is fair game. That's how he was raised. I, on the other hand, came from a family that believed in doing what you want as long as nobody gets hurt. Neither of us recognized that many of our differences were cultural, and it wasn't until years later when I read about the in-groups and out-groups[16] of Greek culture that I began to understand why he believed as he did.

Because cultural differences are often misunderstood, we get frustrated and even angry when others don't *get* what seems so obvious to us. We believe implicitly in the cultures we are part of, especially those learned very young, and we feel like they are part of us. We believe in heaven and hell because our parents told us so; we believe it's a "dog-eat-dog" world because that's what our fathers said; we believe that we must go to church on Sunday because that's what the priest said;, we think of ourselves as democrats or republicans because our fathers and/or mothers were democrats or republicans. And it doesn't even matter that these may mean completely different things today than they did when our parents were young.

I've learned over the years that, frequently, the beliefs we are most passionate about, the ones we defend to the death, are handed down to us through our cultures.

---

[16] Broome, Benjamin J., "*Palevome: Foundations of Struggle and Conflict in Greek Interpersonal Communication*," from Intercultural Communication: A Reader, Seventh Edition by Larry Samovar and Richard E. Porter, Editors. 1993.

We did not think the ideas through; just accepted them without question. We think that our culturally acquired ideas are "natural" and that opposing ideas are wrong and even unnatural. When we get into an argument over such ideas, we are unable to look at the other side with our reasoning minds because we've never even looked at our *own* side that way. We are emotionally attached to these ideas, and we stop thinking when they come up in conversation.

Once again, we *must* be right, and because many cultural mores are part of our core beliefs, we cannot separate ourselves from the ideas, even if, never having considered another perspective on the issue, we have no idea what we're talking about. Our ideas of what's good and what's evil are largely taught to us, and we rarely take the time or make the effort to think past the cultural gatekeepers resident in our own minds. It's too hard, and it can be painful. It can also cause a lot of arguments among our friends and families. It's easier to keep the peace and stick to the beliefs that were handed down to us. That way we can continue to feel good about ourselves, knowing that we are on the side of right.

Can Cultures Be Good or Bad?

There are some cultures that teach us prejudice, hatred, selfishness, and worse. For instance, what if you were brought up in a mafia family? The stuff of your childhood stories will probably not be *Goldilocks*, or if it is, it's likely that the hero of the story is Papa Bear, and Goldilocks definitely doesn't get away unharmed.

What if you're taught from the beginning to respect power, to take violent action when wronged, and to love only your own kind? Such cultures teach fear and breed sociopaths.

Middle-class America tries to instill the basics of compassion and empathy in its children—*How would you feel if all the kids were teasing you? Listen, little love, you have to share that toy with the other kids in the sandbox.* However, at the same time, American subcultures may be teaching the full gamut of fear, prejudice, and hatred, and breeding conflicted individuals who don't know which way is up.

Can we judge different cultures and call one better than the other? All cultures hand down fears of one kind or another: fear of other people; fear of religion; fear of love; fear of women; fear of men; fear of sex; fear of freedom. Pick any human behavior whatsoever, and it's probable that a culture exists that hates and fears other cultures exhibiting such behaviors.

So here is the question: We know that culture is taught, and the endless variety of cultures that exist tell us that it's possible to teach almost anything to human beings. So if culture is taught and people can be taught to be sociopaths, then it follows that they can also be taught compassion. Maybe, like everything human, compassion or sociopathy come easier to some than to others, and age limits may apply, but it's possible that all of us can learn to see with the eyes of love.

Us and Them

Good and evil are part of every aspect of our lives, but if we start with the assumption that we almost always think of ourselves as good, and that in cultural groups we don't even question the rightness of our learned beliefs, then we have to wonder where evil comes into it. Who is evil if we are all good?

Evil starts with the concept of "us and them." It's always this way. *We* are good, and *they* are evil. The first step in making war on another nation is to set them up as evil. *They* are krauts, gooks, ragheads, savages. *They* are bent on evil and destruction, while *we* are bent on peace, progress, or some other named good. By calling names and separating them from us, we are able to dehumanize them and their culture, create negative stereotypes, make them less than human. We do this with words and images.

We start with names. Then when we've created the group, we give it characteristics. This group is evil, greedy, selfish, stupid, short-sighted, ensnared by the devil, kills babies, rapes nuns, hates *us*, and will destroy us if we let them. There's no limit to what people in pursuit of power over others will say to create an enemy, so they can use our fear and hatred of that group to make war and gain their objectives.

When we've done this—named and created a foe—we can then shoot them, kill them, torture them, set them on fire, enslave them, take their women, steal their land, or any other unholy thing we can think of. The first step in every war is to make the other side "them." That way, no matter what we do, we are on the side of good.

And we do this at home too. Our leaders use this knowledge of human motivation to divide and conquer. By playing on our fears of the "other," they are able to gain, and then stay in, power. It goes on all the time, and it goes on everywhere, even in our homes and offices, but especially in politics. By demonizing those on the other side of any issue, leaders can pull their base into a group known as *us* that is against *them*.

They start with a name. For instance, corporate interests do not want the national forests closed off to logging, so they begin by using the power of the press to turn environmentalists into "tree-huggers." This makes them sound slightly ridiculous. Then they take pictures of these people sitting in giant redwood trees trying to stop the chainsaws from cutting them down, so everyone can see just how ridiculous it looks. Add in some commentary by Joe Lumberjack about how they're not letting him work and a couple of jokes by a news anchor, and presto, a legitimate concern for the environment and for conservation, never mind the right of the public to enjoy these national forests, becomes a joke on the latest late night talk show. It's frightening how easily people can be manipulated by putting them on the side of *us* vs *them*.

Not only do politicians do it; advertisers do it too. Remember those commercials about bad breath where two people are talking about a third? Well, there you go. Which side do you want to be on? On the side of the two people who use ABC breath mints and have good breath and plenty of friends? Or on the side of the one who is all alone because he doesn't? The audience chooses the side of the two who use the product without a qualm because no one wants to be alone.

Divide and conquer has many faces, and it's impossible to look at all the ways it's used in this small space. However, just because people use these tactics to define who is evil and who is not, does that mean that there is no real evil?

This is where I have trouble. I would like to say that there is no real evil, only definitions that we make up, or which are handed down to us. But what can you say about Hitler, or genocide, or child abuse? Despite a desire to dismiss all this, it's nearly impossible to do. Hitler killed millions of people in the cause of power. Yes, he did think he was right, making the 'tough' decisions on his way to creating what he considered a super race: blonde, blue-eyed Aryans, who were, in fact, everything he was not. Short, dark haired, unattractive, Hitler was a man who, at his root, hated himself. Yet, whatever he was, whatever he felt, no matter how tortured his childhood, how can he be forgiven? No one has that much compassion. I'd like to say I could, but truly, I can't.

I do understand that that is why I'm still on this earth, and I still have lessons to do. I know there is no absolute definition of evil because it's all dependent on what's gone before and on what will come after. Perhaps Hitler was a scourge that had to be so that the Jews and the gypsies would leave their ghettos and join the world. Maybe those who abuse children have been abused themselves and cannot help themselves because they truly do not know what they're doing.

Still, it seems to me that most evil can be ascribed to those who take power over others. They say that power corrupts and absolute power corrupts absolutely. But we all need power to survive; it's as necessary as air. We all need the power to do things—to get food and shelter. But those who survive on the backs of their brothers do so by taking power that is not theirs to take, and they do it by exploiting the fear inside all of us, the knowledge of our own weakness. That theft of energy is, perhaps, where evil truly begins. Sometimes, this power is given freely, as when we decide in our later years to join a particular church, giving that body power over us. But if power is taken by manipulation, domination, coercion, and theft, it cannot be considered good. I don't think that the end can justify the means.

But who can judge another? Certainly not I. Perhaps, in the process of growth, it was necessary for humans to create large groups led by people who use the power of the many to build the civilizations in which we live. Like single cells joining to become a multi-cellular organism, maybe power must be used in this way before we can reach our full potential. So, though I personally think that *taking* power over others is wrong, I do not believe I have the right to make this judgment.

In fact, that may be our worst failing as human beings, this idea that we have the knowledge, the wisdom, and the right to judge others. We cannot. We cannot know what any other person goes through, and we cannot know what the outcomes of events will be. How then can we set ourselves up to judge another human being, let alone whole cultures?

And yet we do, and sometimes we must. Sometimes, we must look head on at good and evil whether we like to or not.

Religion

They say that religion and politics should be avoided as topics of discussion, and it's true because on these topics, few people are able to reason. Religion is composed of learned cultural beliefs, learned responses, taken on faith and reinforced by our families. These beliefs *must* be right. This need to be right, regardless of what anyone else thinks, makes these subjects extremely volatile. It was neither my intention nor my desire to talk about religion here, but I find that in a discussion of good and evil, there really is no way around it.

When in power, the Catholic Church killed tens, perhaps hundreds of thousands of people as heretics. Anyone who questioned the tenets of the Church—scientists, wise-women (called witches), Protestants, Jews, and Moslems—was in danger, especially while the Inquisition reigned. When power moved into the hands of the Protestants, they returned the favor, burning and slaughtering Catholics.

Taking their lust for blood beyond the gates of Europe, Catholics led the crusades, sending soldiers and knights into the middle east to rape and pillage Islam. Today, Islam, in revenge for hostilities begun a thousand years ago, has declared what they call "holy war" against the infidel.

Somewhere in any family tree, if we go back far enough, we all have ancestors who were raped, burned, stabbed, enslaved, shot, hung, tortured, and murdered, all in the name of somebody's religion. (Although religion is sometimes just the face on real issues of money and power.) Nevertheless, the human race is grasping, violent, and cruel when inspired by fear and greed. On the other hand, when inspired by love, we are kind, generous, and noble.

Christ said (or at least they say he said), "Turn the other cheek," and he urged us to "love thy neighbor as thyself." He was a pacifist. Yet, in Matthew and again in Luke, he says that he came to 'bring a sword rather than peace.'

This contradiction is very startling, and I think it's important to remember that we have no Gospel according to Jesus. Only the hearsay of his followers, which as we all know, is inadmissible in a court of law. Hearsay is not allowed in court because it is unreliable, yet some of us take this particular hearsay very literally nonetheless and without wondering why there is no Gospel according to Jesus. He was educated; he could read and write. Where are his own words?

Nevertheless, given the nature of Christ's mission and the overall context, scholars generally take this quote about bringing a sword to mean a sword as metaphor rather than a literal sword, and certainly not as a proposal to make war.

I brought this up because there is only one tactic that brings peace in the face of violence, and that is passive resistance. To stand before an enemy and turn the other cheek is the greatest act of courage, and it's the only act that has ever made an enemy turn away in disgust at his own behavior. This strategy, advocated by Jesus, was used by Ghandi and Martin Luther King to right great wrongs in their respective countries.

Arguably the most powerful religion on earth, Christianity was led by a pacifist, yet his words and teachings have been twisted and used by those who claim to follow him, to make war, promote violence, grab power, and step on the already downtrodden. I see no excuse except ignorance, greed, and fear. How do we dare to use his name to promote division, and still call ourselves good?

So in defining good and evil, we must come to the conclusion that we are lost in a maze of contradictions. Those who do understand and ask us to live on the side of good, are frequently assassinated or otherwise disposed of. Christ, who most assuredly understood peace, and even had the compassion to forgive his own murderers, was crucified, and then his words were used to promote the violent, grasping ends of the powerful.

Empathy and Compassion

In the end, it seems to me that the best way to define good and evil is in terms of compassion. This too exists on a continuum. There are empaths at one end - those who are accustomed to going through life trying to get into the shoes of others, to feel their feelings and understand their thoughts, and at the other end of the spectrum, there are those who have no compassion at all.

Such individuals live entirely inside their own heads and have no knowledge of what it means to touch another soul. They live in a world where they are all alone and unable to feel any sense of connection to others. Because their survival is wholly dependent on themselves, such souls live in terror. As they see it, there is no one to help them. If they falter, they die. Thus they don't worry about other people. *Let them worry about themselves*, they think. *It's a dog- eat-dog world*. Unable to cross the divide separating each of us from each other, they cannot reach out in compassion to another human heart. But that doesn't mean they can't see or understand other people. Some are very good at it, and many people, lacking compassion, are good at conning people, or worse. They may be responsible for many of the ills of this world. Some are very rich and powerful.

Empaths, on the other hand, exist at the opposite end of the continuum, and feel everything that others feel. At a party, the nervousness of every person in the room becomes a problem for the empath. Because an empath feels your pain, it's important for him to help you. An empath will take you in, nurture you, and spend money on you. True empaths want nothing in return; only the peace of being with a peaceful soul, and they are sometimes taken advantage of by sociopaths because, feeling the loneliness and fear, empaths will go very far to show the sociopath he's *not* alone.

Because, like all oppositions, these two extremes exist on a continuum, there are endless gradations between empathy and sociopathy. Most of us live somewhere between the two: we can feel the suffering of others, but we also keep up a barrier that prevents our compassion from getting us in trouble.

Can compassion be learned? Some of us are compassionate from birth, and the circumstances of our lives teach us to open up even more. Our mothers teach us to wonder how others feel and some of us take this very seriously. On the other hand, others might have the gene for compassion (if it exists) but never meet with a single event that activates it. Their mothers do not tell them to question how others feel, and it never occurs to them to wonder.

Perhaps it has to do with the initial human bond. Those who bond with someone early in life will activate the compassion gene, but those who are left alone and never make that connection, may never learn how.

Whether such a gene exists or not, we can see that the first bond we establish as an infant is the foundation of our compassion. We bond with someone (mother, father, sibling, uncle, aunt, adoptive parent) and learn eventually to love that person. This love, this relationship between self and other, is our first experience of what it means to be human. Through this connection, we experience love—all aspects of love as both noun and verb. We are the object of love, the loved one, and eventually we learn to become the lover as well. Through this bond, we build love, the relationship.

Out of this swirl of confusion between self and other that goes on during our early years, we learn to become ourselves, separate and distinct from our loved ones. But we take with us and keep as part of ourselves, the compassion we learned when we were both one and two.

Sex and Death

When life first began, death only occurred by accident. The first life was single-celled and reproduced by division, creating a long string of perfect replicas of itself. The millionth generation of "daughter cells" was exactly the same genetically as the original "mother cell." But then a new development came about and two cells learned to divide and share their DNA with each other. This original "sex" was also the beginning of death. Now, the mother and father cells would no longer reproduce themselves exactly. Only half their DNA would be passed on to their offspring.

Thus death began. Instead of reproducing by simple division, when human beings reproduce, they share DNA. Neither partner is reproduced faithfully; each offspring gets half its DNA from its mother and the other half from the father. Our children are separate and distinct from us. Death, it seems, is the price we pay.

While sexual reproduction provides greater variety in offspring, it also leads to individuality, and being an individual separate from the mother, is the re-enactment of the moment of separation between the sea of all possibilities and "I am." In this instant, fear is born and out of fear all the sound and fury that is the way of our world.

My best friend in high school was very large. She was funny and smart and at least 150 pounds overweight. Once, I was sleeping over her house, and as we lay across from each other in the twin beds in her room, she told me how when she was a child, she would get these inexplicably high fevers and go into convulsions. With the fever would come a dream, always the same dream: She dreamed she was the only thing. Nothing else existed. She was warm; it was dark, and she was big, very big, encompassing all of existence. Then in a harsh and bitter moment, everything changed. She was small; it was cold and bright, and she was tiny. She was not the only thing, just a small separate thing, and she was scared.

The hairs on my arms stood on end as I listened to this story because I understood it immediately. "You dreamed of being born," I said, and she thought about it before agreeing. I realized that my friend's overweight had to do with this terrible birth trauma. She was always trying to fill up the space around her, to be the only thing once more.

The point is we all go through this terrible moment of separation, and for some of us it's more traumatic than for others. In this moment, however, fear is born in each of us.

We need fear. Fear protects us. It's a tremendous over-simplification, but you could say that when we traded immortal life as a single cell for individuality as a multicellular organism, and cell division for sex, fear became our constant companion.

Fear breeds all the ills of the world. Fear is the progenitor of suspicion, hate, anxiety, jealousy, and anger. Those who fear build walls, hate those they fear, reject other cultures, trample on the weak, grow contemptuous and arrogant, steal power, and make war. Fear sets culture against culture, brother against brother, country against country. Fear may exist to protect us, but it also makes this beautiful world into a living hell. Where then is redemption? How do we make the world safe for each other and for love?

When we're very young, and we begin to separate from our mothers psychologically as well as physically, we develop egos. Our egos are our walls. Ego is the part of us that says "I am," our awareness of ourselves as separate from the rest. Ego is our individuality and our fear of being separate. It is also our defense.

In the name of ego, we all make mistakes when we're young. In our adolescence, we may hurt people we love as well as strangers, take when we should give, renounce when we should accept. In the name of ego, we may break hearts, steal, spy on, even kill. Ego makes us vain, makes us think we're better than we are, and better than others. Ego makes us ambitious for power over others. Ego makes us strive for control. And when ego runs the show, we can do wrong. We can even do evil.

It's when we realize that we've done wrong and understand our responsibility and guilt that we can begin to become what we really are. Not ego. Not separate, but part of the whole that is life. When we understand that there is no real separation, only cultural boundaries and fear, we can begin to live in ways that can change our lives as well as the lives of others.

When we see that we've done wrong, that we have been arrogant or selfish, when we recognize our guilt and see that we have made ourselves separate by our refusal to love, then we can give something back to the world and begin to build a better life. One that is bounded by love and compassion, rather than by fear.

Fear and Hope

We live inside a house of mirrors—perceptual mirrors. What we imagine inside this house becomes our reality. When we are afraid of being used, being foolish, what people think of us, losing money, face, self-esteem, or anything else, we will see with the eyes of that fear, and the results will be as evil as we can imagine them to be. People will hurt us, laugh at us, take from us. In fact, all that we fear will become our reality. When we fear that we will not get what we desire, that becomes our reality.

This section is not about fear and desire, however; it's about fear and *hope*, so before we go on, we have to look at the difference between them. Desire is a much more powerful emotion than hope, yet they are related. Desire is that niggling, wiggling want that can push you into action (the devil made me do it) that you may have to rationalize later. Hope on the other hand, is not so direct. Hope is the expectation that what you desire will come to you. We aren't driven by hope as we can be by desire, and hope, unlike desire, doesn't make us do things we shouldn't.

Remember the story of Pandora's Box? Pandora was the first woman, and Zeus gave her a box and told her not to open it. (Hmm. A lot like Eve and the tree). Pandora, of course, being human, opened the box, letting all the evils and miseries fly out of it and into the world. But she was quick enough to trap Hope inside where it could be harnessed. Hope is a great and powerful gift.

As long as we fear something, we will live with it. If we try to run away, it will follow us wherever we go. But when we face our fears, stand up to them, refuse to let them rule us, they disappear. The way to begin facing fear is to hold in the heart and mind the hope of its opposite. Instead of suspecting that the world is out to get you, simply hope that it supports you. The more you hope, the more often you will find that you are right, and when that hope finally becomes belief, it will also become the truth.

Once, I studied acting in college, and I had terrible stage fright. I was afraid I would mess up, be embarrassed and humiliated. I suspected the audience (other students) wanted me to fail. But then the professor made a little speech and pointed out something I found very profound: When we are on the stage, the audience wants to participate in the magic. The audience wants us to succeed: to be good enough to move them to tears, laughter, and greater understanding of themselves and others. I decided then and there to assume that most people wish us the best and those that don't, will, once they know we wish them the same. This has proven over the years to be true. All right. Not all the time, but often enough. Hope is the first step on the way to fulfillment of all our dreams.

The Way of Love

Good and evil, right and wrong. It is in the midst of this opposition that we are most sorely tested. We want

Spirals: The Connection

to do good, but often have no means of arriving at what that is. In fact, as we've seen, we rarely think about our behavior without rationalizing either before or after we take action. So once we've understood the mechanisms that form belief—cultural hand-me-downs, fear and desire, us and them, compassion or lack of it—what do we do? How do we make choices in our lives?

There is really only one answer. We cannot use our intellects to make decisions because we cannot see beyond our own need to be right and beyond the cultural beliefs that we've acquired. We cannot always trust authorities to make decisions for us because it gives them power that we should keep for ourselves. How then do we choose?

While desire guides us toward what we need and want, and we need to find the way of freedom, we know from sad experience that *license* is not freedom. Desire must be brought into compliance and used to our betterment. In similar fashion, fear must also be tamed. We cannot continue to let it rule us. There is only one way to find the balance point between these two, and to stay out of the clutches of our ability to rationalize anything: When in doubt, we must learn to think with our hearts. To hear what is right from the voice that wells up deep down, the voice that is not a voice. Knowing that we can never give too much as it is always returned to us from the source, in choosing the right road, we must find the way of love.

Let's look at an example: Suppose we are in a quandary over whether to keep the job we have or look for a new one. The job we have is boring and doesn't pay enough, but it's steady, and we can depend on it. We have no idea what the new job is as we haven't found one yet. Should we look or just stay where we are?

This is a pretty simple question, one might say. *There's no path of love.* But isn't there? If we don't love the work we're doing, we're not doing the right work. Look at it this way: There are only 168 hours in a week, and about one third of those hours are spent sleeping. So we have 112 hours a week to live our lives. Of those 112 hours, roughly twenty-four are spent shopping for food, preparing food, and eating food. That leaves eighty-eight hours. Then we have to spend time cleaning ourselves and our houses. If we have kids or pets, we spend hours keeping them clean too. In the end, if we have a couple hours after work to enjoy our lives, that's a lot. Forty hours is a big chunk of time, and life is too precious to waste doing something that bores us. The path of love leads us to look for a job that makes us happy, that fulfills us in some way. So definitely, we should make the attempt.

Or what if we're the CEO of a corporation with hundreds of people on the payroll? Our advertising is missing the mark, being informational rather than manipulative, and we are falling behind in our profits. Do we change the method, join the club of Madison Avenue manipulators, or look for something else—maybe a better product? The easy way is probably to change our advertising and make people buy our product by using their fear and weakness against them, and we can rationalize this, tell ourselves that we need to do this so we can continue to support our people. But, as Spock told us when he gave his life for the crew of the Enterprise: "The needs of the many outweigh the needs of few." It is better to do right than to add to the miseries of the world.

Or suppose we're just an ordinary person, and we see that a huge offshore oil spill is decimating the wildlife in the Gulf of Mexico. What can we do? Go out into the streets and blame the oil company or the government? How can we? Accidents happen. It's our demand for oil that has pushed oil drilling into the Gulf. It's our perpetual need for gasoline for our cars. Yet we don't give them up. We bemoan the results, but we go on driving. Why don't we ride our bikes? Take a bus or a train? Why don't we stop using plastic (which is made of oil)? You know the answer as well as I: because that would be right, but it wouldn't be easy.

Or suppose we're like Jenny. She and Mark were in love, but Mark has left Jenny behind and formed a new relationship with someone else. Heartbroken, she refuses to let go. She waits for Mr. Wonderful to return home, but when he does, it's only for a day or two to see the kids. After a few years go by, Mark is no longer a part of her life, but she still waits for him. This is not the path of love. Jenny thinks it is because she rationalizes her hurt away, telling herself it's just temporary. He's just doing something he has to do. When he's done, he'll come home. Love is real. So he *must* come home.

Then one day, Jenny realizes that it's not going to happen. While she thought he loved her once, it wasn't the true love she dreamed it was. And when it became too hard for him, he left. Now, having looked at this truth, Jenny can begin to see beyond this relationship. And what does she see? She sees the gateway to the path of love. This path leads directly through the truth, into the heart, and through the heart into greater Truth. It is the only way to see right and wrong because it does not involve rationalization.

Hearts do not rationalize; hearts feel. When they feel pain, they cannot do anything but suffer. So, if we let it, the mind takes over, looking for ways to rationalize the pain away or to distract the body. But if we don't let it; if we suffer the pain and move on, we can begin to live authentically once again.

I know this story well because it's my story. I was stuck in this rationalization for more years than I care to count. And although I didn't stand still—I worked; I created; I raised my children—during all those years, my heart was so broken, I could not see the path of love. I loved my children, my family and friends, and my work, but I was always, always grieving for this loss.

Then I wrote the story down and relived it, and what I wrote was true, but when my best friend read it, she said, "He never treated you very well, did he?" And it hit me that he never had. Why was I surprised that he'd left? He'd always been leaving me. Always returning, but always leaving. He never did take care of me or tend to me in any of the ways that lovers care for their loved ones. I was able to look the truth in the face, at last, and start living again. And because I could see that I had created most of my own pain by refusing to see the truth, I was able to finally forgive him, to see him not with the eyes of my fear, but with the eyes of compassion.

So now I begin to hope. I hope that I will be doing the right work in the right place and will happen one day on the right man. And if my hope is not realized, that's all right too because I will still be doing the right work in the right place, and it will be enough.

Hope is the beginning. It is the gateway to the path of love, the door to compassion. On this road, miracles can happen to me…and to you. On this road, we can change the world.

Fifth Spiral: Good and Evil
Dramatic Connection: Motivation
Chakra: Heart
Core Lesson: Hope

We can go through life looking for the worst in ourselves and in each other, or we can open our hearts and learn to see with the eyes of our souls. We may not even believe that we can be loveable, but we must learn to act from hope rather than from fear. As we believe and behave, so will we become.

THE SIXTH SPIRAL

Freedom & Responsibility

The Plot

How does knowing that life is an endless, infinitely related, interconnected whirl of whirling spirals, help us to live better, more effective lives? At the beginning of the spiral is self and the primordial conflict between self and other, between "I am" and the sea of all possibilities. This tension is the bridge between opposites, the power that structures the universe. At one extreme we are the stuff, the material, of life; at the other, the principles that mold that life.

Thus we are both the artist and the 'clay' with which the artist works. The 'clay' we are given is a body, an intellect, relations with others, talents, desires, humor, inborn knowledge, and the abilities to learn and to take risks. We use this 'clay' to create a life, making choices and incorporating the results of those choices, like threads, into the tapestry of our lives. Every event which comes into our lives, however briefly, can be included, or not, into the work of art we are in the process of creating. Every choice we make is an artist's choice—will this add to my work or not?

When we live our lives creatively, making of them works of art, we accept responsibility for each of the choices we make, regardless of how those choices turn out. We recognize that our lives are works in progress, and understand that we cannot fail. Failure, we realize, is when we give up and go live someone else's life. As long as we are working on our own ideal, we are successful.

Making Choices

"To thine own self be true," means no less today than it did hundreds of years ago when Shakespeare wrote it. We cannot truly live any other way. Though we may sacrifice ourselves for our loved ones, we must make that choice in full awareness that it is a choice, and let go of it when it is no longer our choice. When we sacrifice in order to get; when we hold on though we should let go; when we give because we're afraid not to, we only end up hurting ourselves and very often those we want most to help.

We are given this life to work with, to create out of our present incarnation some meaning and, perhaps, beauty. We can appreciate and be grateful for what we've been given, or we can cry that it's not enough and waste this opportunity to achieve and to grow. We make a choice—to take or not to take responsibility for ourselves—and that choice is what makes the difference between the victims and the victors.

Within the structure of western society, we are free to make whatever choices work for us and just as free to make choices that don't work for us. We can choose not to take responsibility for our lives; we can choose to blame our parents, or our spouses, or the political-economic machinery, and whatever we choose, our lives—our works of art—will respond. The consequences of our choices are the details of our lives.

This is, perhaps, a hard and heartless way of looking at things. After all, we don't often make choices in full awareness of the results. No one can be aware of what *will* happen; no one knows how events will turn out. We each live in darkness when it comes to the future. Furthermore, there are social forces at work over which we have no control, and economic influences that force us into roles we may not want to play.

This doesn't mean that we should shrug our shoulders and leave it all up to 'fate,' however. Though we cannot see what is coming around the bend, and we may not even be aware of, much less in control of, the social restraints upon us, we are still capable of a range of choice in how we behave.

For instance, if we're careless of the feelings of others because we feel no one cares for us, that's a choice. We choose to be careless of the feelings of others. If no one then cares about us, that's a consequence. We didn't choose the consequence, the destination, but we did choose the roads we took in getting there.

What if no one cared about us first? What if we were born into a family of selfish people? What then? How can we be responsible if no one ever cared for us? Fortunately, we are responsible. We don't have to look back, thinking we are doomed to loneliness and isolation. We can simply work on today, take the road today that demonstrates that we care, and on these roads, magic can happen and often does.

Whether we are victims of the consumer society, the patriarchal glass ceiling, racial and religious prejudice, stereotypical perceptions, or the veritable blizzard of advertising through which we try to find a sustainable path, we cannot make a single change in the way things are until we first take responsibility for ourselves.

Being alone, being scared, being unhappy, being poor—these are all choices we made. No, we may not have made these choices wittingly, in full knowledge of what we were doing, and it may have seemed at the time, as if we'd had no real choices, but if we look really closely, we will see that we did have some options. Perhaps the only choice was one of attitude, nothing more, but attitude alone can, and often does, keep us afloat when we might have drowned. Regardless of the limits of my choices, I can, at the very least, learn how to control my attitude, turning it from negative to positive. For instance, if someone calls me and insults me, screaming at me for whatever reason, I can choose to stay calm or to retaliate in kind. The difference in the outcome will be as night and day. If I retaliate, I will find myself in a war. But if I stay calm, I can resolve the issue, usually in a way that works for me as well as the other.

The only way we can change the outcomes of our old choices is to make new ones, and to take more responsibility for ourselves. Live as if you have everything to give, as if you are happy, as if you are rich, as if you are brave, and healthy and that will become your reality. When it becomes your choice, it eventually becomes your life.

Spirals: The Connection

The greatest freedom we have is the ability to choose what we will do with ourselves. The negative idea people have about this response-ability, has caused many of us to refuse responsibility for ourselves, and thus, directly resulted in much of the world's misery. Many of us think responsibility means accepting some burden. But think of this:

Responsibility—the ability to respond—is power!

When we are able to respond to what's happening around us, we are able to make changes happen around us. One night, I was in the Ladies' room at the movies, standing in a long line, waiting my turn. I was third in line, and after a wait of ten minutes, the woman at the front announced that only two stalls were operational because the others didn't have any toilet paper. She went into the first booth and started handing out paper to the people standing in line, and suddenly four booths, formerly not in use, were back in action.

This woman saw the situation and was able to respond to it. She took the responsibility and the initiative and got the line moving, solving the problems of fifteen waiting people. This is a very simple example of what we're talking about here.

Taking responsibility for our lives simply means learning to respond to our problems in constructive ways. In the same way that this woman saw the situation, grasped the problem and solved it, we respond to our lives and solve the problems we find there. Like a good mother, we take care of ourselves and everyone around us, asking for nothing in return. This is the greatest power we have. And power, remember, is experienced as confidence and self-esteem.

If it's so easy, why doesn't everyone just do it? Why do we wait until there is absolutely no other option before we respond and take our power? Why do we blame our mother, our father, our husband, wife, boyfriend, girlfriend, school, television, culture, political representatives, and everything but ourselves before we finally say, "enough," and start to respond to the life resulting from the choices we've made or that have been made for us?

Humans are creatures of habit, and it is far easier to do what we've always done, to think as we've been taught to think, and to act as everyone else acts than it is to change. It takes effort to take responsibility and, if we've never done it before, we may have no idea how empowering it is. It's easier to do nothing, when we don't realize that by doing nothing we're missing out on everything. The difference between the life of an individual who is able to respond, and the life of one who hasn't grasped the full meaning of responsibility is the difference between winning and losing. When you take responsibility, you can never lose.

If I were to blame someone else for some aspect of my life, I would, essentially, be giving the responsibility for my life over to that person. I might say it's my husband's fault that I never finished college or that my career is in the dumps, but as long as I make him responsible for my life, I am powerless to change my life. When I decide I've had enough, and choose to do whatever is necessary to make my life into what I want it to be, I have taken back my power and am now able to do what I want with it.

No, it's not always easy. Some of the people we've given responsibility for our lives don't want to give it back. Power over other people does corrupt, and people who are used to owning your power may want to keep it. But, while power over others corrupts, power over self enlightens. When we take power over ourselves, we free, not only ourselves, but those who were formerly burdened with our responsibility as well. As we loose them from the corruption of power over us, we also set ourselves free.

Finding the Balance

Everything in the universe is in balance. The whirling spirals of life we've been discussing result directly from the tension between opposites, whether those opposites are up and down or me and you. When the pull in each direction is in balance, evenly distributed, opposites dance and the spiral begins. When it's out of balance, the dance is skewed, plodding painfully along like a washing machine with an unbalanced load.

All of nature maintains this balance without effort except it seems, for human beings. We see not the balance, but the opposites, not the harmony but the conflict. Obsessed with the "I am" side of reality, we forget the importance of the rest, and our lopsided pace deadens our senses, and blocks out joy.

The conflicts we work within are part of what we are, for, in this life, we see in dualisms. We are taught to do so from a very young age when our culture teaches us things like, "The opposite of cold is hot; the opposite of happy is sad; the opposite of giving is taking." If we were to think about it, we might wonder at the truth of these statements. Cold and hot do not only exist as independent states of being—over here is cold and over there is hot. Rather, they exist as extremes on a continuum of temperatures, and cold gradually becomes hot as heat is applied.

< ——————————————————— >
Frigid – cold – comfortable – warm – hot

The same is so for happy and sad—if grief is at one extreme of the mood continuum we might go from there through feeling sad, to feeling mildly depressed, to feeling okay, to feeling nothing, to feeling content, to feeling happy, and ultimately, to feeling joy. We can feel happy one day and sad the next, but both of these extremes of feeling exist on an emotional continuum like the temperature continuum, and when we get out toward the extremes, toward the edges of experience, we discover one extreme within the other. Cold, at the furthest extreme, burns. In the midst of grief we find joy. The core of hate is love. Pain can be pleasure and pleasure, pain.

When someone we love dies, we learn about grief. Contained in it is all regret. Our hope for the future is blackened by it; nothing exists but the agony of separation. Yet in the midst of war, when loved ones are dying all around, people seek out connections and love, and find it. The greatest orgasm may be the one that makes us cry. We cry at weddings because the joy is so intense it's almost painful. Most murders involve crimes of passion because hate is love that is twisted out of shape or which has been frustrated beyond bearing. Responsibility and freedom are one.

Nothing in life is black and white— it's all in color—and the dualisms we tend to think in are caused by faulty methods of perception. On the one hand, every duality exists on a continuum; opposites are an illusion. On the other hand, beneath every duality, hidden in its heart, is a joining of supposed opposites. It's exactly as if we were to extend that continuum, that line, all the way around, until it meets in a hidden fold of reality. We cannot see the joining if we look with our eyes, but we can if we look with our spirit. Those who live on the edge—who traffic in danger—are trying to get the experience of those joinings, to know the sorrow in joy and the joy in sorrow, the death in life and the life in death.

Extremes of human nature are, in reality, joinings of dualisms, expanding our awareness into wider realms of knowledge. When we go all the way to the extreme and give everything we've got, we must begin to take because there is nothing left to give. When we go all the way to the other extreme and take everything that is, there is nothing we can do with it but begin to give it back. It is the dualisms that create the balancing act that is life, but joy is found in the joinings. The tension must remain, for that is the structure of life, but duality must be bridged, for that is the reason for living.

Though we rarely have names for the continuums of life, only for the opposites, it's important to become aware of those continuums, and to go even farther, and see all the way around, to see the spiral. These one-isms are the vortex through which we travel into the realm of spirit and touch upon joy. Every one-ism is a spiral in the center of which is self, and self, never forget, is the universe.

The key to change is learning that all dualities, including freedom and responsibility, are one. Consciously choosing the details of our lives, we turn our lives into grand adventures. No longer do we plod through it, lopsidedly wobbling round the dance. We move with grace amid even the lowliest burdens.

If your life is not what you want it to be, consider that life is a process, and nothing happens simply because we want it to happen. Though it is imperative to believe before change can occur, change will not occur simply because we believe. For most of us, it also takes effort. We have to show that we believe by acting as if our beliefs are true. This takes power. That power is your will; and that will is born in the decision to take responsibility for yourself.

This is not always easy. As we mentioned earlier, sometimes those who now own your power won't want to give it back, and you may not want to relinquish power over others that you own. Also, there are some powers that belong to the system, the institutions of government, commerce, and culture which create the framework of our lives, and these are not easily changed, if at all, by individuals, except when working in concert.

An even more common difficulty, however, is in getting to the place you want to be before the time is right. There is an order to the universe, and though we have access to the sea of all possibilities and we can tune into it and produce great changes within our lives through it, this doesn't usually happen overnight. Sometimes it takes years of effort; years of learning what we need to know, years of experience. A friend of mine started a business two years ago, his seventh or eighth such venture over a period of fifteen years, and this business finally started to pay off. He said to me, "It's true, the universe will give you back whatever you put into it, but believe me, you have to put a helluva lot out there before it begins to come back to you."

But is that all? What about when you've found the right path and you're doing your right work? The fact is, when you're following your deepest desires and letting life happen, it takes on whole new dimensions, and things happen as you need them to happen. Everything gets easy.

While God does "help those who help themselves," we sometimes help ourselves into situations we aren't meant to be in. For instance, the friend I mentioned above made a lot of money in this venture and became very arrogant about it, claiming it all as his own achievement rather than recognizing the universe of love that made it happen for him. In his arrogance, he took advantage of people. This sparked resentment, and before long, his bookkeeper had absconded with his entire bank account. He was out of business.

This is not because divine will was against him. It was because he let his ego take over, and did not take responsibility for the people around him. Instead of loving them for helping him make his dream come true, he used them, and was treated in kind.

The Tree of Life

Wisdom comes slowly. We may know at a very young age all there is to know about life and the universe, but we may not be able to put it into practice until we mature, until all the many aspects of us are ready and willing to take the high road. We grow into the man or woman we imagine ourselves to be through a long and sometimes painful process, going through stages that lead us toward our goal. These stages exist all at once in our consciousness at a holistic level, but we proceed through them in the sequential patterns of our days. Within a seed is the full-grown tree, but it takes years for that growth to be realized.

As a child we live on a physical level, we know what we need and want—warmth, safety, food, hugs and kisses. We live in the moment. We experience life without awareness of time, existing at the center of self. We could call this the seedling phase. Later, when we grow a little older we add respect, importance and belonging to these physical needs and our perspective, which once centered only on us, now expands, in this sapling phase, to include social relationships with those around us. Here we are much concerned with appearances and little concerned with what's beneath the surface. Teenagers are generally at this stage, experiencing life very visually, seeing only the outsides of people and things.

When we approach a sexual/political viewpoint, blossom phase, we begin reaching out for deeper, more intimate relationships; we open ourselves to learning compassion. Like blossoms on the tree we attract what we need to grow and reproduce. As we've already seen, love and power are very nearly the same thing, and the sexual phase is also political in that it involves power relationships. We often find ourselves, at this stage, in conflict between the need for power and the need to be close to another human being. We work at our careers at this stage, and we work at relationships.

At the philosophical stage, where experience begins to bear fruit, we expand our awareness to include the sharing of our knowledge with the rest of the world. We feed the world with what we've learned, the fruit of the tree, and our need for power may be satisfied at this stage as we give what we've learned and gain the respect of those around us.

In the religious stage, we see that human beings cannot be the center of everything. After all, the universe exists without any help from us. Here we can no longer ignore the fact that winter (or death) approaches. As our beautiful leaves fall away with the cold winds of autumn, we begin to question our beginnings, and spread our branches upward, looking for a higher power to take responsibility for our lives.

At the spiritual stage, we become the seed, holding the knowledge of the tree within our minds, recognizing that that higher power is within as well as without, manifesting our lives as we want them to be, and sharing the knowledge and compassion we've learned. This spiritual self is carried through the winter (death) to be grown in the fertile mind of our new self in our next life, or in the minds of others in this one when the opportunity arises.

Most of us go through many deaths and rebirths during our present lives—death of a parent, divorce, loss of a child, change of occupation. These disintegrations and re-integrations urge us toward wider awareness, opening us to greater knowledge and spirituality, and offering opportunities to share what we've learned with those we touch.

Extending out from the center, which is self, into these successive spiral arms or phases, we grow as human beings, becoming better and better at what we do, learning new lessons in order to mature in wisdom and compassion, or repeating old lessons on new levels in order to grasp a wider truth. We are all potentially aware in all of these aspects of self at all times. Thus a child can have spiritual knowledge, an adolescent can philosophize, and a young man can become a priest. It is, in fact, possible to be aware at all these stages at once, to reach beyond limitation and consciously grasp the whole of our connection to the whole, but rarely are we able to remain in that state of mind.

Some of us choose not to go through all the stages, staying stuck at one or another for long periods of time, sometimes whole lifetimes. This is a choice. Some people stay stuck on the physical, never reaching beyond themselves into the social. Such people are children, always concerned with self, never quite aware of any other reality. Though these people may move out into the politics of the world, their first interest is themselves; they have very little compassion for others.

Some people stay stuck at the social phase, never reaching beyond appearances to the sexual, and though they may have sexual relationships, these affairs are superficial, and often based on what other people think. On the social level we are aware of our connections to other people, but not of our responsibility. If we feel any compassion at all, it's very limited.

Many people stay stuck at the sexual/political stage, making love and power relationships the center of their lives, unable to see that there is more to life, and never reaching out to the wider knowledge of philosophy where compassion includes not just those close to us, but all humankind. At the sexual/political stage we are always relating to other people, but we are focused on ourselves and unable to give for long periods unless we are also receiving. The philosophical experience, however, teaches us that we are servants of a cause greater than ourselves, and it is here that we can put our knowledge to work for the greater good—a political goal that is beyond politics.

Some people never reach beyond philosophical understanding to the religious where a higher power is recognized and our relationship to it explored, and some people never reach beyond religion to the spiritual where that higher power is recognized as both self and other, and all of life becomes as important as self.

Living Creatively

All of us go through all of these stages eventually however, these whirling expansions of self, learning and growing through our experiences in this world over lifetime after lifetime. These stages are not horizontal, one building on top of the next; rather, they are vertical, expanding rings of consciousness surrounding our spiritual core. Like the rings of tree bark that show the years of the

Spirals: The Connection

tree's existence, these stages mark our growth in awareness.

This is evolution and we are all heading toward the spiritual level, the outermost spiral, where the boundaries between God and self are erased, and we are drawn back to the center of the vortex. Awareness at this, the spiritual level, gives us choices we never had before, and makes possible whole new adventures in understanding..

When we are aware spiritually, we know ourselves at all stages. We have seen and understood ourselves as children, as adults, as sexual beings, and as human beings, and we have incorporated this knowledge into our lives. Spiritually, we can see that we have no limitations other than those we place upon ourselves. Spiritually, we can see that we have purpose and that we are capable of fulfilling that purpose, and spiritually, we know there is nothing to fear.

In spiritual awareness, we recognize that responsibility is the greatest gift we can give ourselves. When we take responsibility for ourselves, we take power. That power gives our lives meaning and purpose. People who take responsibility for themselves are those who have accepted the power to make a difference in their own lives, and often, that of others. In spiritual awareness, we travel the right road in our right mind. We give love to everyone we contact and are able to manifest our desires into reality.

People who refuse to take responsibility, or who have never been taught how to take responsibility, become victims. Their lives have no plan and they founder under circumstances that they cannot control. The more responsibility we take for our lives, the more free we become; and the greater our spiritual growth, the finer our responsibilities.

Growth is a creative process, an art, and we are the creators. If we want to change our position in society; if we want to change our lives; we have to grow. We do that by taking on more responsibility and by expanding our awareness.

For instance, let's look at Laura and Jeff. Laura is unhappy in their marriage. She has two young children who make innumerable demands upon her. She never finished college because she got pregnant, but she always wanted to do something good in the world. Her complaint is that her husband doesn't help out. He doesn't really care about her, just himself. She thinks about taking a job though she knows he won't like it, or even about getting divorced. Jeff is working hard every day at his business and doesn't understand Laura's anger. He gives her and the children a good home. He spends as much time as he can with them. What else does she need from him?

Laura needs to take on more responsibility. First, since she has children, she has to recognize what a wonderful, and short-lived, responsibility that is. If she takes a longer view, she'll realize that in just eight to ten years from the day they're born, they'll be largely independent and even able to lend a hand.

Those ten years are the most wonderful and important in that child's life and Laura has the power to fill them with joy as well as responsibility and love. That doesn't mean she has to be with them every second. It means she has to make sure they are cared for every second, even when she's not there. Don't get me wrong; I'm not saying it's easy. With two children whom I've raised by myself, I know exactly how hard it is, and how slowly those ten years can go. The step, I've found, that takes us from misery when our children are young and dependent, to happiness, is called responsibility.[17]

---

[17] For me, the sanity saving device was a piece of paper and colored chalks. I began a whole new existence as an artist while my

Second, Laura has to take care of herself. She has to work toward her purpose in life, which, while it includes her children, may not only be her children. Maybe she can begin by starting college classes at night. Maybe she can get a part time job where she can help people. If she doesn't need money, she could volunteer for any one of hundreds of organizations. As she takes more responsibility, her awareness will grow and she will move out of her narrow existence and into a wider, more purposeful one. She may have to work hard to get Jeff to give her power back to her, but once she achieves that, she's on her way.

When Laura takes this responsibility, besides the wonderful things that will happen in her life, something even greater will take place: Her children will grow up strong and loving and will bring her joy when she's old. They will not be juvenile delinquents. They will not do drugs or go to jail. This is because they will have learned from their mother that their lives have value and that they can direct those lives onto the paths they choose. This knowledge will give them power.

Wherever you find yourself in this world, there is a way to move beyond it. If you can imagine yourself somewhere else, you can change your circumstances. It isn't enough just to think about it, however. While we first have to imagine it, we also have to do it. If the belief is there, the opportunity to take action will arrive. The more we act in a way that supports our belief in the

---

children were small. I kept my work on the countertop and in between the diapers, breastfeedings, crying, playing, and fighting, I found time to color a little here and a little there, eventually discovering that I had some talent. When my children scribbled on my work, and they did, I found that even the worst scribbles can be incorporated into art.

goodness and love of the universe, the more those beliefs will manifest into our lives.

Sixth Spiral: Freedom and Responsibility
Dramatic Connection: The Plot
Chakra: Throat
Core Lesson: Joy

This is the heart of the story that defines your life. Live creatively. Make choices that turn your story into one in which you are successful, happy, and full of joy. Live as if this is the very first day of your life, the day you get to choose only that which is right for you. And then define all that which has gone before as a necessary prelude to this joy. There is nothing to regret.

THE SEVENTH SPIRAL

Ease & Dis-ease

Epiphany

We can live without love; we can live without money; we can live without new cars, clothes, and shoes, but we can't live without our health. While it's true that doctors, hospitals, and insurance companies can keep our bodies alive for years despite our ill-health, such a situation is not one any of us would willingly choose. Disease is no friend to the human race. It does not purify us or make us stronger or make us better people.

Why, when it is so wrong, is there so much of it? Why did my mother suffer for eight long, painful years with kidneys that no longer worked? Did she deserve it in some way? Did she choose it? Was there something she was supposed to learn? My mother was a kind, sweet woman with a heart of gold and a great deal of compassion, and while I do believe that we choose the circumstances of our lives, I cannot believe that she ever chose to be ill. Her illness was an accident, the result of too many antibiotics, too much faith in modern medicine, too little exercise, and poor eating habits. I guess, as much as I don't like to admit it, these were choices she made.

I don't, however, believe she planned to be ill for eight years in some pre-rebirth conference. I don't believe she intended to die and we, mistakenly, kept her alive. While there is order in the universe, we are not destined to fulfill our lives in some predetermined way. We choose the circumstances, the framework of our new life, but not the details. These are left to happen as they will. Thus there are accidents and mistakes, and nothing is ever perfectly determined for we do have free will.

Disease is the result of such an accident, for health is the normal state of affairs. Most of these accidents can be prevented though simple maintenance and care, but there will always be a few that we are powerless to avert, and these, while they probably teach the victims little, should, at least, teach the rest of us compassion.

I did a terrible thing just before my mother died. I went to visit her and she was feeling very depressed. She looked at her arm, covered with bruises, cuts, scars, and pinpricks and puffed up around a permanently inserted tube, and said, "I used to have beautiful arms . . . ?" I agreed with her and went on to say how her shoulders were also beautiful once and her neck and her face, but now she was still beautiful around the eyes. I don't know what I was thinking. Perhaps I was a little impatient, tired of her being sick. It would have been so easy for me to say,

"You're always beautiful to me, Mommy," because she was, but I didn't.

Two days later, when she was dead, all I could think was that I had let her go with those selfish, inconsiderate words. No matter how sick she was, she was still a woman, wanting to be beautiful to those she loved.

Our compassion is tested every time someone we love becomes ill and sometimes, as I did, we fail the test. Perhaps this is the purpose of illness then—to help forge the compassion of others. If, however, we don't choose to teach such lessons, we should begin to learn to keep ourselves healthy. Only by taking responsibility for our own health can we take the steps necessary to prevent accidents from overtaking us.

It's like owning a car: if we take care of it, it will be ready when we want to go somewhere.

It goes without saying that tobacco, excessive drinking, and drug use damage the body and make accidents more likely. There are enough threats to our health in our polluted environment without adding more, and if we are addicted to any of these substances, it's a good idea to let go of them as soon as possible. I used to smoke three packs of cigarettes a day, and I know how difficult it is to quit, but it can be done. In fact, if I did it, anyone can. It took me over a year of trying before I finally hit on a method that worked. I made a vow. I said, "God, if I ever smoke another cigarette you can curse the rest of my life." That worked. If nothing else has worked for you, this might.

Emotion and Health

According to Dr. Candace Pert, former head of Brain Biochemistry Department of the National Institute of Health, emotion is not located in our heads but in our entire bodies. In fact, emotions, caused by short amino acid chains called peptides, can be lodged in any organ, in the glands, or in the nervous system.

While receptors for every type of emotion are found in certain areas of the brain, different emotional memories and mood states can be stored anywhere in the peptide network. This means that an emotional memory can be located in the pancreas, or the heart, the liver or the large intestine, where it can be accessed in any number of ways.

For instance, if you have a memory that has to do with food and eating, you might access it through the pancreas by eating the types of foods that stimulate the pancreas to produce insulin. It may be that feelings of parental love are stored here and that's why some of us tend to eat sugary foods when we're down. Or an odor, by stimulating certain peptide receptors located in the nose might set off a powerful memory that causes us to react, not just to the current odor, but to the past one as well.

Unexpressed emotions are literally, then, lodged lower in the body. Nothing becomes truly conscious until the whole body is involved in understanding and integrating the experience, and Pert tells us that emotion—in the form of peptides—travels up from the periphery of the body through the spinal column to the brain where it can then become conscious. The brain, however, in an attempt to prevent overload, actively keeps emotion from reaching this stage. This, Pert suggests, is the cause of illness. Emotion must be expressed, must be felt, and must be spoken yet the brain may not allow that to happen:

> There are levels of integration. You are integrating lower brain areas when you move the emotion up and get it into conscious-

> ness. That's where you begin comprehension . . . . A woman . . . reacts to spilling scalding coffee on herself by being startled and feeling pain. The emotional reflex moves up and up and up the body. When it finally gets to the level of the thalamus, [the lower brain], she says, 'Oh, it's hotter than it usually is . . . .' It's only when it gets all the way up to the cortex, [the higher brain], however, that she can actually blame her husband . . . . (Candace Pert)

Raw emotion is always moving up the spinal chord while the need to resist it is coming down from the brain. Pert suggests that emotion must be allowed to 'bubble up,' to the brain where it can be spoken of, in order to complete the process of moving it out of the lower body where it can cause illness.

That unexpressed emotion can cause illness is nothing new. Psychologists have been saying so for years. What is new is that there are biological facts that support this view. We've long believed that stress can cause illness, for instance, but what is stress? In Pert's terms, it is the struggle between the brain and the body—the need to express emotion and the need to keep it down. It isn't always feasible to express how we feel—feelings, especially of anger, are often quite uncivilized—so our brains rationalize and tell us we don't really want to kill anyone. Unfortunately, that deadly anger stays in the body where it will, eventually, kill us.

Emotional Expression

Given the choice between repression and expression of negative emotions, repression is usually the wiser—or at least, safer—course, however, there are other possibilities. In fact, there are many ways to positively express emotion and maintain health including dancing, painting, exercising, writing, studying, learning, meditating, psychoanalysis, yoga, acting, singing, loving, and daydreaming.

We can release stored emotional energy in any activity if we bring the emotion to awareness at the same time we perform the activity. Thus, we can exercise and remain as uptight as we already are, or we can exercise and allow ourselves to feel what we feel at the same time, finishing our activity feeling physically fitter and emotionally more satisfied than when we began.

For example, when I got divorced, I was angry all the time. When I exercised, I would punch the air, pretending it was a certain man. Now, I know this is not very 'new age' of me, but it worked. I cried, screamed, broke things, and punched the air and eventually came out on the other side of that emotion. Sometimes it helps to use a pillow and beat the bed. Whatever it takes, if something terrible has happened and you've got a lot of anger inside, it's better to release it than to keep it inside.

In fact, if you feel anger towards your mother or father that you don't understand, anger that goes back to your childhood, this technique will work. If you really let go, you might even remember what it is that you're so angry about. Hit the bed, call it by the person's name, and say how angry you are. Keep it up until you don't feel that way anymore, even if it takes weeks to get it all out. When you can begin to see that person's good side, you'll know you have succeeded.

Not all repressed emotions are so violent. Sometimes we repress love because it's inappropriate to express it; sometimes we just push down our annoyance at all the little details of everyday life. For me there are two techniques, which are in fact related that release emotion and balance the body, mind and soul. These are meditation and Hatha Yoga, and we can do them either separately or together.

Yoga is physical and it aligns and balances the body, tightening muscles, stimulating the endocrine system, and stretching and strengthening the spine. As a physical activity the benefits of yoga are dramatic. If we do it regularly, after a few months we find ourselves walking with the grace of a dancer, our movements silky as we glide across the floor. But the benefits of yoga don't stop at the physical; that grace carries over into all the aspects of life. As we are centered in our bodies, we become centered in every other area as well.

Yoga is often done in conjunction with meditation. In fact, the purpose of getting our bodies into such wonderfully balanced physical shape is to make it possible to meditate without interruption from the body. When our bodies are uncomfortable, it's hard to keep our attention centered. Yoga trains the body to composure so that the mind can attend to higher things. Whether through yoga or not, meditation allows us to relax so thoroughly that the emotions locked in the body can be released without any effort at all. We simply let them go, release them into the air and let them be carried away from us.

Meditation involves using proper breathing and the imagination, first, to release negative emotions, and second to access the creative mind. Meditation can affect our physical health, but it can also affect the way we move through life. When we are centered and free of negatives, we embrace life more fully and give to it more graciously than otherwise. In turn, this positiveness in our lives attracts more positives and life gets better and better. When we aren't buried under our own fear and anger, it's amazing how pleasurable even simple things can become, and how much more easily we laugh.

Sometimes the emotion lodged in the body is not negative but positive. For instance, when I was a child, if I were really upset my mother would give me ice cream. This would quiet my fears and anxieties, and today, when I'm very anxious, if I eat a bowl of ice cream I feel better. In fact, if I eat any kind of sweet, I get a feeling of relief—my mother loves me, and I'm safe.

It is very difficult to let go of this feeling. Why should I let go of something that can calm me so easily? Unfortunately, sugar addiction is as dangerous a habit as tobacco addiction, leading to overweight, hypoglycemia and, in extreme cases, to diabetes. If we want to keep our bodies healthy and prevent the accident of disease, we need to let go of all emotions that determine how we behave, not just the negative ones. Food is a drug for many people and if our eating is in any way out of control, there is probably a bottled up emotion behind it.

The American diet is notorious for its high sugar, high fat, and high salt content. Each of these is a deadly killer, and many of the diseases we observe are the result of diets high in these elements while lacking in fiber and high quality nutrients. It's important to eat well, that is to eat whole grains, fresh fruits and vegetables, necessary fats only, and to use sea salt and avoid processed sugar.[18]

Finally, I want to say a word about doctors. The medical establishment does not know everything there is to know about the human body, and while doctors are very good on diagnosis, the only treatments they

---

[18] Any health food store will have many books that will tell you the kinds of foods necessary to maintaining your health.

know are drug therapy, radiation, and surgery, all of which are powerful and dangerous. Be very careful about the drugs you take; all drugs cause side-effects. Penicillin, for example, can cause near-sightedness. (Is it any wonder that so many of us wear glasses?) Taking too many antibiotics can turn your body into fertile ground for drug resistant bacteria and make you more susceptible to disease, and certain antibiotics can cause kidney failure. In fact, there are some people who go to doctors and get sicker and sicker, not because they can't get well but because the drugs they are taking affect other systems, and they end up more ill than when they began.

I am reminded of a television movie starring Meryl Streep, *First Do No Harm*, in which she portrays the mother of an epileptic child who is almost killed by his drug therapy and who finally is saved by a special diet. This was a true story (it happened to her neighbor) and there are many like it that never reach the screen.

This is not a how-to book and I've barely touched on some important techniques for the maintenance of health and prevention of accidents. There are books, videotapes and classes available on yoga and meditation, as well as books on diet and health. If any of the techniques I've suggested here are attractive to you, I urge you to study further.

The Balance Between Happiness and Disease

Like everything else we've discussed, the body itself exists in the balance between polar opposites, in this case happiness and dis-ease. The spiral is defined by two forces pushing against each other and forcing the flow into a circular pattern. If one force moves outward the other pushes inward. One is the thrust, the other the limit. Thus water can fall downward, but when it hits the bottom (the limit) it begins to spiral. It's the same for flesh. Soul falls into flesh (its limit,) inspires it with life, and the spiral begins.

The force is joy. The limit is flesh. If we were to experience only joy we would explode our boundaries. If we were to know only dis-ease we would cave in and collapse. The balance that keeps the molecules of life spinning out their webs of relationship is somewhere in the middle. That's why it's so important to avoid excess. Even the best of what we do taken to excess is damaging. For instance, I know a woman who believes in exercise. She believes in exercise so much that she sacrificed everything else, including husband and children, for it. She has great shoulders and a beautiful, trim body, but at forty her face looks sixty. Bitterness, jealousy, and anger are all written there.

Between happiness and dis-ease are contentment, honor, integrity, commitment, respect, purpose, and dignity. Walk your own road, define your own path, accept the consequences of your actions. Understand death. Relinquish fear. Give love. Physical health is the outcome of healthy emotions.

Belief

Beyond the physical is a state of mind, a system of belief that is responsible for the state of our consciousness and of our health. As we grow in awareness, as we learn who we are, we begin to understand that our ability to choose goes very deep. We can choose what to do and what not to do. We can choose what healthful habits to take up and what to leave behind. But more than that, we can even choose what we believe. As we have seen, all things exist within the sea of all possibilities, the source of our lives and power. Our truth today may be just a small part of Truth. Because of this, we can choose from within this sea to believe in those parts of Truth with which we want to live.

If we believe in the power of illness over health, we will one day succumb to that power because it is based in fear. But if we believe in the power of our bodies to maintain health all their days, we will be among those who live to ripe, healthy old age regardless of our habits.

I personally believe in health over illness, but for me, it comes with a sense of *deserving* health through right action. I am still working on this, and one day I hope that I can eat ice cream with as little care as I now eat carrots.

Epiphany

I have seen that we have a choice and that we do not ever have to choose illness when we can choose health. We do not have to believe in illness. We can look at ourselves and at others and see in them the divine perfection from which they are born and in which they exist. And when we look with these eyes, illness cannot be. It is only when we see with the eyes of our own narrow-minded and fearful egos that we are limited by dis-ease. Our natural state, in God's mind and being, is perfect. See only this in yourself and in others, and perfect health will be yours.

Seventh Spiral: Happiness and Disease
Dramatic Connection: Epiphany
Chakra: Third Eye
Core Lesson: Faith

Yes, this is what it comes down to: Let go of fear; have faith in God; believe in the perfection that is you and everyone else around you. The results will be exactly as you would expect: divine.

THE EIGHTH SPIRAL

God and Self

The Climax

At a subatomic level electrons spin around their nuclei, weaving patterns of energy around a central core. When atoms join together to make molecules, the paths their electrons travel can get infinitely complex. A ball of wax at this level is a veritable universe mostly made out of empty space. As electrons spin around their nuclei, so do planets circle around suns. As galaxies spin into great double spirals, so does the molecule, DNA, the blueprint of life, present in every living cell, form into double spirals called helixes.

There is a theory that suggests that the universe is like a hologram. If the universe were a photograph, and we were to tear it up into little pieces, each piece would contain the universe itself. In the same way, we, as holographic bits of the universe, are in fact, the universe. We are, at one and the same time, nothing, a bit of minute material floating in an infinite sea—a scrap of paper—and everything, the very universe itself.

At both the microcosmic and macrocosmic levels, everything is spinning. The center of each atom is the center of the universe where "I am" and the sea of all possibilities reach out to each other and circle in their joyous dance, straddling the gap, the positive negativity, that structures all-that-is. This cosmic orgasm constitutes each particle of creation as well as each larger system. On every level the universe pulses, its heartbeat no different in an atom than it is in a human being, in a world, a solar system, or a galaxy.

God is Born

Each atom is alive and combines with others to create the cells that combine to create larger systems, which include us. As we reach the limits of any given system, matter and energy begin to cycle back and forth, thus beginning the spiral. Blood and lymph circulate through the body, emotion creates real physical chemicals that also circulate throughout the body. Thought itself moves through the system, affecting it physically. Words, sights, sounds, and events from outside affect our internal milieu and are returned to the outside in talk or action.

We are open systems, circulating the cosmos through our minds and bodies. In the same way that we take oxygen in and breathe out carbon dioxide, we also take in everything around us, keeping some of it within and spinning the rest out in conversation, in relationships, in work, and in love. These systems, these open, circulating systems, are the interface between that which is within and that which is without, between the invisible center and the visible exterior. At the limit of every movement outward is a movement inward, thus we contain the gap within us and we live within the gap.

The Divine Universe

While at the level of the atom we are touching the center itself, we are, at the same time, not the center, but separate individuals caught within larger, more visible, spirals. Thus, God—meaning the dance of God and Goddess—is both immanent and transcendent. God is both within us and outside us. The divine spark of life, embodied in matter, is wrapped up in the divinity of the universe. Everything is God. There is nothing that is not God.

If we were to examine a whirlpool carefully, we would find that the water isn't just spinning on the surface. It's also being sucked into the center and pulled down where it spins outward and upward, joining once again that surface whirlpool. The eighth spiral draws us back toward the center where it all begins, where transcendent God, the God outside, becomes one with immanent God, the God within, and spins us out again.

Our spirits are divine but so are our bodies, for life is God. The best of us and the worst of us, it's all God. The corruption and the altruism, the ugliness and the beauty, the self and the not-self, it's all God. When we walk down the street, we are walking through the mind of God. When we talk to each other, we are talking to God. When we love another we are loving God. Nothing exists but that which "I am" creates out of the sea of all possibilities, and it is, all of it, holy.

Anything we cannot see as holy is being observed from a limited, judgmental perspective that sees us as separate from each other rather than as connected individuals balanced in the dance. Out of this perspective comes fear and all the ills of humankind. For it's only when we are not afraid, when we can experience ourselves as the interface between the inner God and the outer, that we can truly live.

The Multiple Nature of Truth

Truth is not singular, but multiple. The one Truth is composed of many relative bits of truth in the same way that humankind is made of human beings, and rocks are made of atoms. Any event which takes place in our lives is subject to interpretation depending on our perspective, and it is these millions of different ways of seeing the same event that make up the Truth.

My truth regarding anything, raising children for example, is different from anyone else's—that's why my children are mine and yours are yours—but all our ways of raising children together are the greater Truth: Raising Children. It's necessary to go beyond our own limited truth and try to see a bigger picture. And to contribute our truth to the whole by living in ways that acknowledge that larger Truth.

We must learn to see humankind as one being, each part of which requires care and love. Just as we learn to nurture our bodies with good food, laughter, and love, we must learn to nurture the human race with the same, distributing food where it is needed, knowledge where it's required, and love everywhere.

As long as there is suffering, as long as whole groups of people are used and abused, we will not have reached the perfection we seek, and very few of us will be able to reach into the heart of power and create our lives out of it.

It is not enough to look to ourselves, satisfy ourselves, take care of ourselves. While giving to ourselves is a necessary step in our evolution as human beings, it is not the end, for evolution, too, is cyclical. Human thought brought us to where we are today and human thought, as it reaches the boundaries of its current paradigm, will bring us around to a place similar to where we were before. As we reach the limits of one historical period we return, at least in part—for evolution is not circular but spiral—to an earlier time. Today, as we reach the limits of self-indulgence, we begin to long for the sense of the community we left behind.

We miss the town center and the public square and find little satisfaction of our need to be part of a life larger than our own in shopping malls of the same name which replace them. As we become increasingly isolated by the social structures we have designed to reflect our belief in individualism above all else, we begin to look for other answers. As a result, the spiral turns and thoughts of community begin to concern us. New developments like cohousing[19] begin to appear as people take responsibility for themselves and their children and start to find workable solutions.

Beyond each of us is the rest of us, and while we must be able to attend to our own purpose in life, to please ourselves and to experience the great generosity

---

[19] Cohousing and intentional communities are being created all over the U.S. and elsewhere as people seek closer social involvement in food preparation, maintenance and childcare. For more information check the internet or the library under "cohousing."

of the universe, we must also attend to the greater purpose, and please others. As in everything else we've discussed, the Truth is not found in one way rather than the other way. It is found in the meeting of ways, in the relationships between ways.

Many people suggest that the poor are poor because of the choices they've made, and hold out individuals who have "made it" despite the limitations of their beginnings, as examples of what can happen when a poor person trusts in the abundance of the universe. The poor are poor because of the choices they make, but they are also poor because of the choices made by those around them, the social systems and cultural institutions that maintain the status quo. Those exemplary personages who rise above their circumstances are the strong, the innately powerful, the intelligent, and the lucky.

Children born to poverty may not have a lot of choices. Making it in middle class society is not always easy for those brought up in middle class society, how do we expect it to work for someone whose lifespace has been bounded by drugs, gangs, motherhood at fifteen or younger, and a great lack of all the products so devoutly worshipped on television?

If you think that anyone can make it without help despite coming from this place, picture yourself suddenly dropped into Beverly Hills and ask yourself if you could make it in there. You don't know what the rules are; you don't know the people; you don't have the right clothes or the Rolls Royce; and you don't know how in that world to get them. Where will you make your movie deal? Who will trust you? And how will you survive while you figure it out?

While I am in no way suggesting that we are not completely responsible for what happens to us, because we are, I am suggesting that we are also responsible for the rest of the world. This is, perhaps, a paradox. If we're responsible for others doesn't that mean they are responsible for us? The answer is no. We are responsible for ourselves and for them, but they are not responsible for us. (Well, maybe they are, but before we can see the whole world change, some of us will have to take the high ground and give generously even when no one gives back.)

This doesn't mean we should run out and make every poor person a rich person, because that wouldn't necessarily help. That person might still be poor, only with a lot of money. It means that we should help in any way we can to raise the consciousness of the poor from one of lack to one of abundance by giving such individuals a chance to take responsibility and making it possible for them to be successful at what they do.

We all must believe in abundance for it to come to us. By being generous, we demonstrate our faith on the one hand, and make it possible for people who have never had enough to begin to believe in a generous universe. It is a big responsibility, but if we would change the world how else can we do it? If each of us takes responsibility for that part of the world that impinges on our awareness, we can make progress.

See yourself as a parent. Whether you are male or female, your responsibility is to see to your children—everyone around you—your mother, father, sister, brother, husband, wife, daughter, son, relative, neighbor, or friend. Whatever they are—rich, poor, beautiful, ugly, compassionate, selfish, loving, careless, responsible, irresponsible—or any of a hundred different ways of being, they need your care, attention, and respect in order to grow into the best they can be. If we all give whatever we can, financially, emotionally, and spiritually, we will one day find ourselves in a much better world.

As long as we see ourselves not as cells in a larger organism, but as individuals struggling against each other in order to survive, we will remain exactly that. When the human race comes together, reaching out to each other to give with everything we have, then and only then, will we succeed in knowing ourselves, and begin to make a better world.

It's almost as if we are pregnant with our own potential. Before we can realize that potential, we must perfect each and every cell of our being, both within and without. That is, we must perfect ourselves, and then we must give to each other and perfect our species. When we succeed in obliterating poverty, hopelessness, misery, usury, tyranny, environmental degradation, war, and all the rest of the ills that besiege us, we will have raised ourselves above ourselves and onto a new level of life and perception, where other spirits abide, waiting to welcome us.

This process goes on willy-nilly, whatever we have to say about it. And whether we consciously add our spirits to the effort or not, we are nonetheless, part of it. The world is growing and evolving . . . and we are evolving with it. This *is* the dawning of the Age of Aquarius and out of our growing universal love for each other will rise a new and much improved human race, a human race that recognizes its place within the cosmos, that knows itself to be part of the earth rather than its conqueror.

Surrendering to the Divine

Since all is divine and we are each of us divine, it is the simplest truth that successful living comes out of accepting our place within this divinity. When we understand that everything that exists is meant to be, that

Spirals: The Connection

we are all on a path toward our greatest good, then we can accept with humility and joy everything that comes to us. There is nothing to resist. There is nothing to worry about. There is nothing to do but take what is given, demand what we need from the limitless source of our beings, and give all we can to everyone around us.

Surrendering to the divine is the source of all happiness. Once we have reached this state of awareness, magic begins to happen to us. We have desires that come true without effort. We have issues that dissolve into laughter. Our worries disappear and our loves become the cornerstones of our lives. Ask only this of the divinity within: Give me the love, health, wealth and ability to express myself, which is mine by divine right, under grace in a perfect way.[20]

When all the walls come down, when fear has no place within us, when love inspires us in everything we do, Joy bubbles up, a fountain of light, expanding our awareness into infinite dimensions. Joy is Truth, and Truth is love. Reach inside yourself to your heart, open it up, let all the pain and fear fall away, and what you will find, bubbling out of that connection to the source, is Joy, the ecstasy of being alive. Treasure it . . . share it . . . and dance!

---

[20] Shinn, Florence Scoval. *The Game of Life and How to Play it.* NY: Simon & Schuster, 1986.

Eighth Spiral: God and Self
Dramatic Connection: Climax
Chakra: Crown
Core Lesson: Self-Expression

Surrendering to the divine is the climax of our soul work on this earth. When we do it, we begin to create our lives as they were meant to be. Let your life take the shape you desire most by letting go and letting the universe make it happen in the right way as it's meant to be.

EPILOGUE

Between Madness & Reason

Relativity

Scholars today say that we live in the postmodern era, marked by a lack of reality in our reality. It's what we mean when we talk about our children growing up on video games and television. Think about it. Today, we get up to the sounds of a digital alarm clock, make coffee brewed from beans already ground, eat mass produced eggs, walk down the paved pathway to the car, drive—or take some form of mass transport—to work inside some office, store, or factory where we are surrounded by machines and computers all day long. In the evening we drive through the traffic back to our homes, eat dinner—prepared from a cut of meat purchased at the supermarket—watch television, and/or get on the internet.

On the weekend, we go to the mall, or to the movies, out to a restaurant, or to a nightclub, or to friends' houses. While a few lucky ones get to ride horses, or walk in the woods, or go to the beach, most of us never encounter nature at all, beyond watering the plants and looking at trees through the windows of our cars. There's so much light pollution in our populated areas we have to go to planetariums to see the stars.

We may never have seen a cattle ranch, or a milk cow or a chicken. We don't have the slightest idea how our food is grown. We may never have eaten blueberries off a bush or seen how a cucumber grows. The 'realest' thing in our lives is water, and though we have only the vaguest idea how it gets to our faucet, or where it comes from, we do worry about it being polluted.

This disconnection from nature is, perhaps, the worst thing that has ever happened to us. It is through nature that we discover reality, through nature that we understand the seedling and the fruit, through nature that we observe the cycles of change and growth that are the world, the solar system, the galaxy, and the universe. Living in a world where all we see are reflections of ourselves in the media and in each other, we lose track of who we really are. We get lost in a house of mirrors, and it's no wonder that children brought up under such conditions become violent and turn to drugs. It's madness.

We live in a world where everyone is supposed to find their own truth, where truth is always relative to the circumstances around it. It's not okay to lie, but it's okay if it will help someone. We shouldn't hurt other people but what if they're hurting us? We have lost our center, the wisdom once passed down from generation to generation, which told us that there is an absolute right or wrong; we just had to find it out there. In the postmodern age we believe that there is no truth out there, only what we perceive the truth to be within. We cannot find a center, so we make the center ourselves.

The trouble with self as center is that self is not unchanging and stable. Self is flexible and flowing. Self rationalizes. The spiral has a center but there are a million, gazillion spirals just within us. Never mind out there. Our center one day can be love, our children the next, our work the day after. Where do we find the rock on which to anchor our lives? Where is that one unchanging certainty that settles all questions and gives us direction in all our decisions? Where do we find peace in the midst of all this tumultuous change?

Change is a certainty. "This too shall pass," may be a cliche, but it's also a great truth. We can depend on change. What is today will not be tomorrow. This can be a fearful thought. We don't want things to change. We want things to stay the same. Depend on change? How absurd! But is it really? When we recognize change, and don't fear it, we can live joyfully, in the moment, trusting that whatever happens, it will ultimately be for our good.

It may not seem so at first; who among us hasn't desired one event to take place rather than another, and been bitterly disappointed when it didn't happen? Yet, who among us hasn't, in the fullness of time, realized the seed of good that was in the experience we *were* given? When we accept change, faithfully trusting in the great intelligence of the universe, less time is spent in fear and bitter disappointment for what might have been, and more in joy and gratitude.

The truth is out there, and it's also inside. The center is both the dance within us, and the whole wide universe. When we see it, when we study the external world and begin to understand the cycles of life on every level, we begin to understand how perfect and whole it is, and to know that we are part of it, whether we like to think so or not. The spiral nature of reality unfolds before us as we are ready to receive it.

Want to save a child? Send him to camp for the summer. The change might not be instantly apparent, but it will be there inside him, and it will grow. Want to save yourself? Go out to the woods, or the shore, or the mountaintop, and watch the stars circle around the heavens, observe birds nesting in trees, let an ant travel up your arm and watch what it does when it returns to the anthill. Ride a horse; feed chickens; eat blackberries off the bush. Real, authentic life is out there in the real world, not on the television screen. Go and find it. You'll find yourself as well.

The difference between living life purposefully and just living is inside. All it takes is the flip of an inner switch to turn us on to ourselves, and hence, everything else in our lives. That switch is creativity. When we don't like the circumstances of our lives, what we can do is create different circumstances by making different choices. Each of us is the embodiment of the dance, a reiteration of God itself, a spark of divine awareness. We can make our lives anything we want our lives to be. Not by wishing, not by thinking—by believing and by creating.

First we recreate the assumptions that underlie our existence. Remember, I said we were assumptions carried to their logical conclusions? Our assumptions got us where we are. If we don't like where we are, we have to change our assumptions. As we've seen, Truth is everything and can be anything. It's just as easy, and likely, to believe we are powerful as it is to believe we are weak.

Spirals: The Connection

All we have to do is flip that creative switch and start to give. It's just as easy, and likely, to believe that the universe is abundantly generous with us as it is to believe we will never get what we want. All we have to do is be grateful, act as if it's already true, and create it in reality.

We exist here in this creative moment, and we can do anything we want with it. I can change my destiny in an instant by burning this book, or by leaving my house and never turning back. I can also change my life by deciding to learn something new, or by taking on more responsibility wherever I can find it. I can choose to be jealous of those who have more, and to give nothing because I'm not getting enough, or I can choose to give the best of myself everywhere I can and replace my envy with satisfaction. Choices are out there. We only have to choose to be a better person, believe that it's so, act as if it's so, and we become a better person.

Living is an art. We can master the medium and create something beautiful out of it, or we can pay little attention to the Art as a whole, and get lost in the day-to-day drama of the parts we play. To create a beautiful life out of the raw materials we've been given is a challenge for all of us. It has been said that the Buddha was born walking and talking, and lotus blossoms grew up under his feet. The rest of us, however, have to work to find the middle way. There our lives can flower into the work of art we've created, first in our imagination, and then in the world.

Here are my steps to changing a life; they're very simple. First, stop trying to get anything from anyone. Second, take responsibility for your life. Third, give to everyone around you as if they were your own beloved children. Fourth, meditate on what you want your life to become. Fifth, act as if it is already that way. Do this and miracles will begin to happen. As a dear friend and I once agreed, "it's not getting there, it's being there."

The sea of all possibilities exists now within each of us and all around us. To change our reality, all we have to do is create a new reality out of this infinite sea of choices. In this creative moment, the sea of all possibilities is ours to work with, the paint with which we compose our life picture, the clay out of which we sculpt our form, the words out of which we create our life stories. We should never let the "I am" part of us, the ego, get in the way of our art.

The Goddess and the God dance around each other, loving each other, giving to each other, and that is what we must do within ourselves. When we nurture both our creative, holistic side and our egocentric, sequential side, these begin to dance around each other, trusting each other to hold on. In this middle ground, in the gap between self and the sea of all possibilities, we can use our intuition and our intelligence, our wisdom and our calculations, our love and our desire to create the tapestry of our lives as we would have those lives become.

The spiral is a simple form defined by opposing forces. If we look for it we can see it everywhere, within every aspect of life. From the swirling nebulae of the galaxies to the infinitely small and beautiful spirals of the Mandelbrot set, from raging hurricanes to replicating DNA, from the passing of the seasons to the stirring of soup, from history to drama, the spiral structure underlies all of reality as we know it, and love, the positive negativity at the center of each spiral, is all-that-is. That's why the only thing that really matters in life is who you love and how well you love them.

Give and take, up and down, to and fro, in and out, being and non-being, pain and pleasure—it's all one.

Spirals: The Connection

Imagine the most beautiful thing you can imagine, the most majestic being, the most precious love. Imagine yourself glimpsing the infinite face of God himself in all his incandescent glory. Watch closely as God and the Mother of God, the limitless sea of all possibilities, dance forever in graceful, measured splendor. Watch closely and remember:

Thou . . . art . . . That.

INDEX

actors, 5, 10
authority, 13, 53, 59, 60, 79, 81
beauty, 20, 85, 86, 87, 88, 90, 109, 140
belief, 19, 37, 49, 50, 88, 90, 91, 103, 125, 136, 142
Campbell, Joseph, 16, 18
Capra, Fritjof, 54
chaos, 4, 22, 62
children, 3, 1, 14, 15, 17, 18, 20, 21, 24, 28, 38, 40, 46, 48, 58, 59, 60, 63, 66, 76 - 79, 82, 84, 94, 100, 106, 120, 122 - 124, 135, 141, 142, 144, 148 - 150, 152
choice, 4, 24, 80, 109, 110, 111, 120, 131, 136
Chopra, Deepok, 13
coincidence, 39, 40
compassion, 27, 28, 36, 51, 84, 85, 94, 98, 99, 100, 103, 106, 119, 120, 121, 127, 128
creative, 15, 66, 123, 133, 151, 152, 153
creativity, 151

culture, 16, 45, 46, 82, 83, 85, 87, 92, 102, 113, 114, 117
dance, 10, 14, 19, 21, 22, 23, 26, 27, 29, 47, 51, 54, 57, 114, 116, 139 - 141, 146, 150, 151, 153, 154
death, 9, 18, 19, 31, 32 - 34, 41, 45, 51, 69, 77, 83, 86, 90, 100, 116, 119, 120, 135
desire, 54, 58, 65, 75, 76, 77, 80, 81, 90, 91, 94, 96, 103, 147, 153
disintegration, 49, 51
divinity, 140, 145, 146
DNA, 46, 100, 138, 153
drama, 2, 5, 75, 152, 153
ego, 48, 65, 66, 70, 88, 90, 102, 118, 153
emotion, 56, 91, 129, 130, 131, 132, 133, 139
empathy, 84, 99
environment, 35, 36, 38, 93, 128
epiphany, 4
evil, 9, 18, 75, 76, 77, 78, 81, 84 - 86, 91, 92, 94 - 96, 98, 102, 103

fear, 23, 41, 51, 60, 73, 75, 76, 77, 78, 80 - 88, 90, 91, 93, 95, 96, 97, 99, 101 - 104, 106, 107, 122, 133, 135, 136, 137, 141, 146, 150

feminine, 18, 19

freedom, 77, 85, 103, 111, 115, 116

galaxies, 138, 153

give and take, 55, 59, 60

giving, 9, 10, 56, 59 - 66, 68, 71, 72, 81, 86, 95, 113, 114, 142, 144, 153

good, 9, 25, 28, 33, 37, 55, 67, 75 - 98, 103, 112, 121, 123, 128, 132, 134, 141, 146, 150

happiness, 124, 135, 146

health, 126, 127, 128, 131, 133, 134, 135, 136, 146

hologram, 138

hope, 2, 4, 5, 20, 38, 47, 68, 91, 106, 107, 115, 136

inspiration, 3, 5

intention, 2, 54

Leavitt, Ruth, 17

madness, 149

manifest, 122, 125

maps, 49

masculine, 46

men, 15 - 19, 43 - 47, 63, 69, 70, 82, 85

motivation, 93

nature, 2, 5, 26, 35, 43, 46, 57, 58, 66, 97, 114, 116, 149, 151

negativity, 57, 70, 139, 153

perception, 30, 35, 115, 145

Pert, Candace, 130 - 131

plow, 16

postmodern, 150, 151

power, 1, 9, 10, 19, 45, 53 - 73, 77, 84, 86, 93 - 97, 102, 103, 108, 112, 113, 117, 119, 121 - 124, 136, 142

rationalization, 78, 105, 106

reason, 14, 27, 28, 38, 39, 57, 63, 79, 81, 96, 111, 116

relationships, 10, 28, 44, 46, 52, 55, 57 - 60, 61, 63 - 65, 68 - 72, 119, 121, 139, 143

religion, 18, 19, 77, 80, 85, 96, 97, 121

responsibility, 37, 38, 51, 78, 102, 109, 110,

111 - 119, 121 - 124, 128, 142, 144, 152
sex, 9, 19, 47, 85, 100, 101
taking, 9, 24, 25, 28, 41, 55, 59, 61, 65 -69, 71, 76, 80, 95, 114, 123, 128, 134, 152
Tannen, Deborah, 43

truth, 7, 8, 22, 26, 39, 87, 88, 91, 105, 106, 114, 120, 136, 141, 145, 149, 150
ugliness, 85, 86 - 88, 90, 140
women, 14, 15, 16, 17, 18, 19, 43 - 47, 51, 63, 70, 76, 78, 82, 85, 93, 96

The Healer
by Deborah Greenspan

"... a frightening world gone wrong where the fragile human belief that good can triumph is all that stands between life and the end of the world ..."

Can the future change the past? In 1973, Peter and April find a mysterious baby in their backyard who grows to have amazing healing powers. But when the world discovers him, Josh becomes a potential weapon.

Meanwhile, in the future, descendents of the rich and powerful living in underground Habitats strive to restore the earth, except for John Morgan who wants to rule the Habitats and all those who live in them.

As Peter and April race to escape those who would capture and enslave their adopted son, Morgan carries out his plan to rain nuclear havoc upon the earth, and Evie and Garret, two talented New Scientists who have been Outside, strive to stop him before he destroys all those who still live on the surface. The battle for the earth takes on apocalyptic dimensions across time as ultimate sacrifices are made, and past and future converge in a cataclysmic event that changes the world.

ISBN: 978-1-933626-12-3
200 pages
6" x 9"
Sci-Fi/Fantasy
$14.95

To order from Llumina Press:
www.llumina.com/store/healer.html
orders@llumina.com –
866-229-9244
Available from Ingram, Baker & Taylor, and Amazon

Kids' Day
By Deborah Greenspan

"A great story for kids...and for adults too!" - *Healthy Kids*

A light-hearted romp through a system that's come to a screeching halt, *Kids' Day* is just dark enough to hold up a mirror showing kids how they fit in the world and how that world holds together.

While camping in the mountains with her parents and three brothers, Diana meets Flora, the Roman nature goddess who is tired of being ignored. Flora grants Diana's wish that adults stop working and start playing, and at first, it's great! Mom and Dad are off their cell phones and totally involved with their kids. Okay, so there's no TV, but is that really a problem when DVDs can be had for the taking?

In fact, anything can be had for the taking; that green stuff is just play money! The trouble begins when people start fighting over toys and ice cream in the mall, and escalates to a complete shutdown of electricity, water, medical care, and food supplies. The kids finally decide that people really do have to work, and head out to the mountains to set things right.

ISBN: 978-1-933626-09-3
140 pages
5 x 8
Sci-fi/Fantasy
$8.95

To order from Llumina Press:
www.llumina.com/store/kids.html
orders@llumina.com
866-229-9244
Available from Ingram, Baker & Taylor, and Amazon

www.ingramcontent.com/pod-product-compliance
Lightning Source LLC
Chambersburg PA
CBHW031643040426
42453CB00006B/193